Simpli*fly*

Mark Dias

Human Performance Coach

GeniusMedia
CREATING KNOWLEDGE

2021

Simplifly

Managing your mind's autopilot to create more with less

First Edition: July 2021

ISBN 978-1-908293-60-2

Genius Media 2021

Genius Media

B1502

PO Box 15113

Birmingham

B2 2NJ

United Kingdom

www.geniusmedia.pub

books@geniusmedia.pub

Contents

My Thanks

It's not happy people who are grateful,
it's grateful people who are happy

Mark Dias

I would like to begin by sharing my heartfelt thanks to the following people, without whom this book would not exist, and I would not be where I am today.

My wife and best friend, Poonam, the force behind me, encouraging me to step out of my comfort zones and venture out into areas I hadn't thought of exploring. The one to encourage me to pen down my thoughts for a book. From looking after the kids when I was busy, to doing my share of the chores to free up my study time. Thank you for being you.

My mum, godfather, and sister for shaping my early years, reminding me the world is my oyster and happiness is an inside job. Thank you for your love and providing me with a strong foundation.

Captain David Ray, a true leader and friend, who for the last 3 years kept on telling me, almost every time we met, you should write a book soon. Thank you for introducing the idea of writing a book and more so, believing in me.

Captain Abdullah Nasr Sultan Al Riyami my mentor for the last decade. For opening the door to his knowledge and allowing me to take a stroll inside his fascinating view of life and aviation management. The true master of keeping complex simple and teaching me his learnings from Bruce Lee; that a stiff tree cracks but bamboos bend, that knowledge is power, but respect is in character and knowing is never enough until you can apply it. Thank you for offering me every opportunity to explore my creativity.

Captain Kelifa Hassen, a true friend and mentor, who spent hours teaching me about his passion for automated systems and flight management. My tour guide for life, showing me that you are not your circumstances, and that gratitude is the highest form of being. Thank you for teaching me the functions of the real autopilot, that made me compare it to life.

Captain Adam Sinclair Morris, who I have spent hours of class time working alongside. A mentor and close friend who taught me so much about the world of Crew Resource Management and Human Performance. Thank you for your mentorship.

Peter Freeth and Charles Saldanha, my own coaches who taught me everything I know about Neuro Linguistic Programming (NLP). Your knowledge in this field of study is exceptional. Thank you for your time and guidance.

All my students, fellow crew, and clients, who have shared their experiences, challenges, and stories with me.

Mark

Foreword

Energy always

David Ray

I first met Mark in Dubai in 2008. I was part of a
small group formed to start a new airline. I had just
retired from United Airlines as a A320 captain. 39
years as an active pilot with the US Marines, Pan
American Airways, and finally, United. My wife,
Nancy, and I came to Dubai to visit friends. Our 3-
week vacation turned into a 13-year adventure we
never could have imagined. Mark joined our team and
became a big player in that adventure.

During my vacation I learned that a start-up airline
was looking for a Chief Pilot and Head of Flight
Operations. Long story short – I applied and was
accepted!

My expertise for the start-up team was a strong flight operations background and pilot management experience as Flight Manager for the 1200 pilots of the San Francisco domicile. When I learned that my application to become the first chief pilot was accepted, I was thrilled and looked forward to getting back on the flight deck. I really missed flying. I felt confident and was eager to get started.

Looking back, I realize how naïve I was. Starting an airline and running an airline are two vastly different challenges – the former far more the difficult. Running an airline consists of managing an existing organization. Starting an airline has no such resources. And I had no experience to prepare me for much of what the next year would bring. Fortunately, Mark was on the team. His contributions were vital to create the open communication culture we all wanted, and safety demanded.

One of our biggest challenges was to recruit, train and integrate pilots and cabin crew with a very wide range of experience. Our pilot recruits were highly experienced aviators but often the cabin crew were selected not for experience but for positive attitudes and willingness to learn. Our goal was first and foremost safety. Safety in all aspects of the airline. To achieve this goal, we would need and extensively use the vast skills and experience Mark brought with him.

Although you won't find this term in the book, his area of speciality that attracted our startup airline is referred to as "Crew Resource Management" or CRM. Many volumes have been written on the critical importance of CRM. This science has since migrated to the medical profession. And Mark is one of the top experts in this field of improving communications on the flight deck and cabin – between pilots and between cabin crew.

Mark and his team developed our CRM training program from the ground up. The program is brilliant. I have attended many CRM training sessions with Pan Am and United Airlines and I can enthusiastically say the CRM training Mark delivered is the best I have ever experienced. He has a natural talent for speaking and capturing his audience's attention and participation. He creates enthusiasm and sharing. Hands reach for the sky to add their input or question a concept. Energy always.

I was thrilled when Mark told me he was writing a book. As much as I admired his work with our airline, I could sense he was destined for a larger role. For many years, I actively encouraged him to take his talents to the next level. We had lovely conversations about what the next level really meant. I so admired his dedication to his own education and the improvement of his craft – art really.

I was humbled and honored when he asked me to write the foreword to this book. And, intimidated. I have experience writing on aviation matters – articles, reviews, procedures, ops manuals, presentations, speeches, and more. But never a foreword for a book whose author I greatly admire and consider a friend.

Mark's book is about our life's journey – yours and mine. Mark uses his extensive experience in developing aviation communication training to write a thought-provoking book to help us navigate the challenges and roadblocks of everyday life. His is a timely book that helps us understand and reconcile contemporary differences in thought and opinion.

He starts with a discussion of the aircraft autopilot.

The autopilot is an essential tool for pilots if used properly. The aircraft autopilot is a marvellous modern device for enhancing aviation safety. As Mark puts it, "the introduction of the autopilot was a boon to aviation safety and pilot workload". He is correct. The autopilot, as well as improved communication training, safety training, and enhanced hardware safety systems, have created the safest mode of transportation available today. But the autopilot – like all systems – has limitations.

Mark has used his expertise in aviation communication and safety systems, to bring to us a book that uses this aviation experience to help us navigate our personal circumstances. His book is analytical with everyday life experiences and examples to drive home his points. His illustrations are easily recognized and understood. Each chapter concludes with a list of questions that reinforce his message and helps us relate them to our own lives. I genuinely enjoyed the questions and examining my answers. It was challenging and inspiring. I urge you to read and review the questions carefully.

I have talked about myself and how I came to meet Mark. I have tried to frame the trials that our team faced with starting an airline. Now I want to tell you why Mark is the best person I know to write this book. His lifelong passion and expertise have been to understand human communication and how to improve the process.

In addition to his extraordinary aviation experience and training, mark has a strong and long-standing coaching practice (www.markdias.co).

He wrote this book to blend his world of aviation experience with his passion for coaching and helping people. While his book is aviation-themed, it is fixed on his experience with life coaching. The book is heartfelt and honest. Mark's message is clear, true, and relatable. This is a book you will underline, revisit, and remember. I know I have.

To quote Mark, "The truth is that life can get complicated. Things happen." Mark has a marvellous discussion of the difference between complex and complicated. His book led me to analyze this concept carefully by giving great examples and suggestions on how to deal with the unexpected.

From Mark's book: "This book is about that journey from take-off to landing. You can't control the weather (or many other factors). But how you fly through this game of life is entirely up to you!". And he breaks down the hardships ahead and offers positive thoughts and suggestions to get us back on course.

Mark starts his book with a warning not to rely too much on your personal life's autopilot. He finishes his book, after showing positives and negatives about our personal autopilot: "What if our autopilot doesn't have to be ditched?", he asks. "But just programmed to the right settings?". This book helps us to do just that.

By sharing his insights, he gives us the opportunity to examine our flight path in life. Please read this book carefully, Mark has much to share with us.

I know you will enjoy the journey and your voyage through this book. I certainly did.

David Ray

US Marine Corps (Retired)

Commercial Pilot

Flight Instructor

¹Autopilot

The world is obsessed with telling you to stop living on autopilot. I'm sure you have heard or read the term 'autopilot' to mean mindless living, daydreaming, following your habits or a lack of focus. From meditation teachers to life coaches to your friends and well-wishers, the poor autopilot seems to have had its reputation stained and can be looked upon with a frown in the context of our busy lives.

But wait a moment... What do people like me with decades in the aviation business have to say about the parallels drawn between the real-life aviation autopilot and the metaphor everyone else is referring to? Let's just pause for a moment and question this so-called life on autopilot.

Is it really a bad thing? Could it be used for some good? Or is just that we haven't figured out how to optimise its use in life?

What if there are certain automated ways of being that are best left on autopilot? What if some of them actually serve us in that auto mode? What if the autopilot doesn't need to be d!tched but simply programed to the right seting? What if we had a manuall like pilots do have, to understand how to manipulate and control the autopilot, to make it work for us and not against us?

So before I further elaborate, a quick autopilot check.

- ✈ How many spelling errors did you notice?

- ✈ How did that make you feel?

- ✈ What judgement did you place on me? My publisher? My attention to detail?

- ✈ What conclusions were you drawing?

- ✈ Did you feel this wasn't good enough to continue reading? Did your perfect self feel a bit agitated?

- ✈ Did you go from 0-100 with "Gosh I can't believe this"!

- ✈ Did you speed read and notice no errors?

- ✈ Is your eye for detail just an eye or does it move past that, to judgements and quick conclusions?

- ✈ Did you empathise with me, giving me the benefit of doubt? Perhaps English isn't my first language?

Depending on your answers to the above questions, you should have a decent appreciation of your autopilot setting of judgement and perfection. If these answers opened up some insights and learnings, read on! This book will help you understand the system you operate from internally, by understanding the autopilot (the real one) and the one you apparently are a victim of!

So, getting back to our autopilot... Ask anyone in aviation who understands the functions of an autopilot and you will get a different perspective on its utility. The autopilot has evolved from taking over tedious and energy consuming tasks from the pilot gradually over the last few decades.

The introduction of an autopilot was a boon to aviation safety and to pilot workload. It helped reduce the physical load of holding altitude, speed, making basic turns and kept the aircraft flying from point to point. More importantly, it freed up mental capacity to do other things and thereby reduced workload drastically and kept the pilot free for more important decisions. Yes, yes it also came with full new set of problems, its reliability, its complexity and the need to monitor it! Today systems are so reliable that they have created another level of problems; dependency and skill degradation. The system is so complex with multiple interface levels that no pilot really understands all of the various interactions and interdependencies of the software. There are also a few levels of automation that work within this autopilot, for example at a basic level it will do simple tasks for you and at an advanced level it will do the job literally of another pilot. You need to learn how the system - including he human pilot - works to decide what goes on autopilot and what doesn't. In poor visibility the autoland feature can get your aircraft within the touch down zone of the runways with stunning accuracy! But when you hit a sudden gust of wind close to the ground and your speed or altitude goes up or down, the autopilot often struggles, perhaps even disengages and the human has to take over this demanding task.

When you repeat a behaviour, your brain will automate it for you! The brain in many ways is lazy or, better still, very energy efficient. This makes a great point for pilots and checklists. The routine checklists in the cockpit are meant to protect critical tasks, this is done by stopping what you are doing to read the checklist. One pilot reads and challenges whilst the other responds. Why do they still miss things out? The answer is above! The mechanism the brain comes with will automate the learning and memorise the checklist without your permission. Checklists get executed everyday with willpower and discipline. The pilot despite knowing it on the back of his hand must consciously make the effort to disengage his mental autopilot and read the checklist like it's the first time.

How many times have you gone shopping for food, not written a list because you know what you need, and then come out of the store with everything apart from the thing you went in for?

The brain's autopilot is so effective that it will keep you doing things that are not good for you in the long term, like smoking. It's smart and at the same time a little biased, it won't consider the illness and health risks despite you knowing them – something that psychologists call cognitive dissonance. The prefrontal cortex is a brilliant working executive, it can risk assess, calculate, think, rationalise… but it's like a vacuum cleaner that has a 15 minute battery life, eventually it gets tired and loses to the basal ganglia, the part of your brain which forms and controls your unconscious habits. Habits on autopilot will beat the rational brain with pure persistence. The same holds true with the autopilot and automated systems in the aircraft. They are so reliable that the human gets dependent on it and this causes skill degradation and adds to the high level of dependency. Some experts argue that the rate of error of the automated system is so low that it makes sense to let the human just monitor it rather than trying to do its job. The accuracy and protection the automation on a modern aircraft can give you is stunning, this support is great, but the day your skills are challenged when the system fails, a wake-up call awaits. Regulatory authorities and airlines often require that pilots prove their handling skills in a simulator every six months. This ensures their automated habit of dependency is no longer available to them and puts their prefrontal cortex to work, alongside some handling skills. Otherwise, if you keep on using your autopilot, how do you really know that you can still perform the task? Take an everyday task like making coffee or driving a car. Sure, you obviously know how to do it, but could you really teach it to someone else? Do you know what you know? Would it come as effortlessly to you as you did it when on autopilot mode or would you have to pause, retrace the steps and then respond? Either the task you perform is done with some level of mindfulness, which would allow you to retrace and explain your steps or it was done on complete auto-mode. When your autopilot is engaged, the automated action is difficult to retrace or explain. Your autopilot is taking care of that for you.

In life how does this play out? Do you ever detox your automated habits? Do you retire them and for a day and notice what this does to you? There are a number of autopiloted beliefs, habits and behaviours that lock your identity into a certain mode. When your autopilot is engaged in a mode that serves you well, you automatically move towards a more balanced, restful, even joyful state.

Many people are stuck in a pattern of working towards some future goal or lifestyle. The fact that they are putting their goal in the future means that, logically, they cannot have it today. They say, "Once I get X then I can do Y and then I will be Z". So they can't be Z right now, because they aren't doing what it takes to achieve it. For example, "Once I get a promotion then I'll have the money to move house, then I'll be happy". In reality, the promotion was never the barrier, the money was never the barrier. The belief in the absence of happiness is the barrier! Unless you HAVE something you cannot DO and therefore cannot BE what you want.

What if we switched the autopilot around to work in the other direction?

BE DO HAVE

✈ Who do you need to BE?

✈ What would you then DO?

✈ What would you then HAVE?

Think about something that took you some time to learn, like how to parallel park a car. At first, parallel parking was complex and you had to give a lot of thought to it. There were too many variables, too many things to pay attention to at the same time. But after a lot of practice, it became much easier, and now you might do it without thinking. You consciously set the target, and your unconscious mind takes care of the rest. You set the destination and your autopilot figures out how to get there.

Every autopilot habit forms around a pattern called a "habit loop" which has three stages. First, there's a trigger which sets off the unconscious set of events. Second, there's a routine, like a program which runs. This is the part of the habit which we're aware of, or we can observe in other people. If you have a friend who bites their nails, they are aware of the nail biting, but probably not what causes it. The third stage is a reward, and it's the reward which reinforces the habit. A habit gives you something that you want, so you keep on doing it!

Neuroscientists have found that the habit loop is created in an area of the brain called the basal ganglia, which also contributes to the development of emotions, memories and pattern recognition. Conscious, rational decisions are made in a different part of the brain - the prefrontal cortex. As soon as a habit forms and the autopilot takes over, the decision-making area of the brain takes a back seat – at least for this task. This frees up your mind to focus on more important things. While you're making coffee, or driving your car, you can listen to music, hold a conversation, think about your day ahead. You wouldn't be able to do these things if you were having to pay close attention to every task. You couldn't even make the coffee.

The concept of habit goes back at least as far as ancient Greece. Aristotle explained that "We are what we repeatedly do. Excellence, then, is not an act, but a habit." Hippocrates said, "Make a habit of two things: to help; or at least to do no harm." The idea of habits, good and bad, is seen throughout the popular culture around the globe, including countless articles and self-help books. However, it was not until recently that we understood the structure of habits and habit formation. We have also recently begun to grasp the psychological roots of habitual behaviour.

In experiments conducted by Graybiel, rats were tasked with learning a maze. Graybiel discovered there was a lot of neural activity in the sensorimotor striatum, part of the basal ganglia. However, as the rats mastered the maze, neural activity changed. A group of neurons had been firing throughout the maze run but after habitual learning, the activity in this part of the brain was high at the beginning and end of the run, but quiet in the middle. Habits can then be seen as stored neural patterns, with neural firing at the beginning and end.

Our habits are learned behaviours reinforced by expected outcomes that can take the form of a reward. To change our habits, we must learn a new or different behaviour that would then have a new reward. However, our brains do not like to learn new behaviours when the reward is still guaranteed by the old behaviour. Why change something if it works? You must know someone who performs some task in the most complicated way, and when you show them an easier way they resist and say that they like to do it 'their way' because it's reliable.

So, what can we do to challenge our habits?

Simpli*fly*

When you watch people's habits you'll see patterns. They'll do the same thing, the same way, every time. Think about shaking hands. Once you learned to do that, you did it the exact same way. Shake hands with someone and notice the exact same patter, the same grip, the same number of shakes, the same timing.

Luckily, your mental autopilot, just like the one in the cockpit, has an off switch. Research from MIT shows that the brain's prefrontal cortex still has some control over which habits are triggered, so you can adjust the settings on your autopilot when you have a change of plan or you want to set a new destination.

Habits often become so ingrained that we keep doing them even after we have stopped benefiting from them. It isn't enough to kick yourself when you follow the habit because you're not in control of the trigger and once your habit has been engaged, once the autopilot is on, you're not in conscious control anymore.

Your brain's prefrontal cortex can only stay in control for so long before it loses out due to exhaustion. The basal ganglia can just keep going and going, so if you don't make time to interrupt your habits, they will win in the long run.

What elements of your life are best suited to autopilot? As you go through this book you will discover how you can live with the correct use of autopilot by understanding how your system works. Life really is flight, everyone is a pilot, everyone is navigating, goes through turbulence, ascends and descends through their flight, has technical issues (health, finance), has software glitches (mental health), has to interact with air traffic control (the world around you), your crew (friends, family and colleagues) and passengers (people you serve, your customers and clients). This book is about that journey from take off to landing. You can't control the weather or the passengers you have on this flight, this is not in your hands. But how you fly through this game of life is entirely up to YOU.

Let's prepare for take-off.

Questions

- ✈ Name three things which you can do automatically which your daily routine depends on.

- ✈ Name three things which you can do automatically which you would rather change or have control over.

- ✈ What habits do you have which you have tried to change?

- ✈ What do you think stops you from changing habits?

- ✈ How do you reward your habits?

- ✈ What triggers your habits?

- ✈ How can you become more aware of situations which trigger your habits so that you can plan ahead for change?

- ✈ How can you find other rewards which are more valuable for you?

- ✈ What do you really want in your life?

- ✈ What do you really want out of your life?

- ✈ What are you prepared to give in order to get this?

²Simplify

Life is really simple, but we insist on
making it complicated

Confucius

If you look at a baby, unless they are hungry or need a diaper change they are by default set to joy mode. The autopilot setting is 'joy engaged'. Once they grow slightly older into children, the same joy setting is active to a large extent. If joy is a default setting, how does stress create that default substitute? Stress is an emotion, a response to conflict pressures acting on you and must be felt for some time when needed. Stress can cause you to take action, to get moving. The problem is when it becomes your autopilot default.

The truth is that life can get complicated; things happen. The brain is inherently lazy and likes the quickest route out. But then how does life get so complex, so cluttered and messed up?

When things can be set to the autopilot mode of simplicity, joy, ease, how does that switch flip to overwhelming confusion? This is what I call The Biryani Theory! So in case you are not aware, biryani is an Indian dish made of rice, meat, vegetables, spices, nuts, plums, saffron… the list goes on! A biryani is one of the most extravagant Indian dishes out there. It's complex, utterly complex! In the making and the ingredients; with almost 20 different ingredients, ranging from spices, to meat, to the marination and cooking, you're looking at 2 hours of preparation here. I sat at an Indian restaurant years ago and placed an order for a simple white rice. 20 minutes later the waiter served me a biryani.

What could have been going through the chef's mind? "Rice? Plain white rice? That doesn't sound right. He can't want rice, just rice by itself. The waiter must have made a mistake. I'm sure he'd like a little garlic. Maybe some oil. A few strands of saffron would be great! I know, he's a tourist, he didn't know what to order, he meant a biryani, I'll add a few onions. Maybe some spices. A few vegetables. There! Perfect! That's what he really wanted!"

No, I really, really wanted white rice. In about 10 minutes everything was resolved, and I was united with my plain, simple, white rice. I sat to eat my simple dish and it occurred to me; this experience was so similar to life.

How many times have you wanted that simple white rice, but found yourself cooking up a biryani, or being served one? You see life can get so complex as it is, with managing work, family, self-time, your health, the list goes on… Ever so often our autopilot is set to biryani mode, which is the highest level of complexity and life drama, when all we really need is that white rice.

Whether we call it biryani or pilaf, risotto, jambalaya, nasi goreng, machboos or paella, the theory I have on this is that it is important to choose simplicity over complexity, a play over the drama. Your energy and time are precious, align them to serving yourself a dish of happiness and ease over stress. You see the complexity in a biryani is in the layers, time and energy that go into making it so delicious. But unlike biryani, life doesn't need the intense complexity and difficulty to prove success. You need to put in hard work and long hours, dedication and… what else? To succeed? Is that enough?

Why do people who make it big in life find it hard to admit it was easy? Surely for some it was not, but maybe that's the story they tell about the troubles they have overcome, because nobody wants to read the autobiography of someone who was just lucky, inherited all their money or won the lottery. We want the story to be complicated and difficult because then we feel comforted, it's OK that we don't have everything we want in life. Why does almost every successful journey have to show struggle, patience, failure, disappointment, broken dreams, and pain to finally present success? Have you ever seen a movie that went 'hero has privileged upbringing, finds life easy, succeeds at everything, wins, the end'? No. We want to see people struggle, and we want to know that struggle has an end, that there is a way to rise to the challenge and succeed against all the odds. We want to see movies that go 'hero fails, fails again, gets help, learns important lessons, wins at a price, is a better person'.

Are we programmed to believe that success is only available via biryani and not the white rice? Are jobs and promotions autopiloted to award only the hard workers, hustlers and those who display their ability to navigate and come out of a biryani – even one that was self-created?

It's not just a YOU problem, it's a system problem!

Let me explain.

Years back my wife and I were discussing how a senior manager in her office was on a long vacation, the department that the manager led was in complete chaos! One of the vice presidents made an interesting comment on this chaos, he said, "It's clear this senior manager was key to the business, clearly without him the business cannot function." Now in the world where I come from, the aviation system is built on redundancies, we have backups to support systems and the human! My view on this was the exact opposite, if a department is running seamlessly without the manager, this is a master class on management and leadership. If it's not, you have a problem, a rather big one that shows a system being built solely on one pillar, one unreliable, unpredictable human pillar.

You see the old view of macho leadership and chaos management that requires the leader to be present is still part of the world we live in. Yes, leaders need to take charge and show up, yet the most productive ones are almost invisible and don't need to shout about their achievements to prove anything. The white rice leaders encourage simplicity, structure and build their team on the autopilot settings of joy, responsibility, creativity, ease, energy conservation and management.

Ask yourself… Am I within a system where I am rewarded, only when I can prove I can deal with complexity? Am I programmed to create complexity only to surface victorious? Is a simple story that delivers success too understated for the world to buy into?

In no way am I suggesting that complexity is not part of life, the aviation industry and many others works in a system of changing odds, multiple layers of complexity, numerous factors that join together like a puzzle to create safety through reliability and predictability. A few dominoes can line up to knock each other down. A biryani can fall on your lap without any effort too, when that does happen your default autopilot setting to creating simplicity and structure will be of more use to you than ever.

There is a big difference between complex and complicated. Yes, life can be complex, systems can be complex. A mechanical watch is complex. An aircraft is complex. Thousands, even millions of components, all designed to work perfectly together. But humans are also very capable of taking simple things and making them complicated. What's the difference between 'complex' and 'complicated'? They're obviously very similar words. Complex means that a system has many interconnected parts. Complicated means that someone made it that way.

We all have to deal with unexpected situations in life, and we might for a moment be startled, surprised, shocked or scared. Training and life experience teaches you how to deal with these surprises. The first time you experience a shock such as an accident, your unconscious brain takes over to protect you. You jump out of the way of the approaching car, or you reach out to stop yourself falling, or you pull your hand off the hot stove without thinking. In fact, you can't think, at least not with your rational, knowledgeable, logical neocortex. Older, simpler parts of your brain have taken over to protect you. Your reaction to a threat is built in from birth. These threats turn into stress when you can't react to them, when you are trying to deal with conflicting demands from different directions. Over time, you get used to this, even addicted.

The problem is when stress becomes your autopilot default. Through life, you learn a default mode, and maybe you learn a default mode for different situations. One for home, one for work, one for family, one for friends. In your childhood, you are surrounded by adults who want to protect you by telling you how complicated and difficult life is. You start to worry about what other people think, you try to predict what other people will do or say.

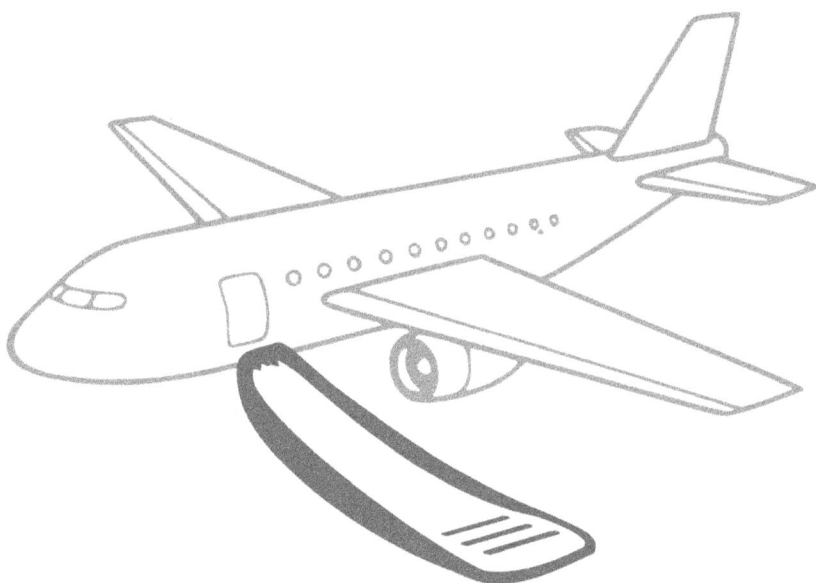

Years ago I sat in a meeting with an airline I was doing some work with, in this meeting the fate of a cabin crew's future employment was being decided. She had made an error, by deploying an evacuation slide (inadvertently). This is not only an expensive error as a slide if damaged can cost over US$30,000, but in addition the delay of replacement, which has a knock-on effect to the next flight that aircraft needs to operate. In worst cases, if the aircraft is at full capacity and a new slide cannot be arranged, passengers would have to be offloaded as an emergency exit is inoperative, and this domino effect can carry on. Clearly a big error!

So how is it fixed? Easy, terminate her services and the problem has gone away. It took close to three hours to decide it was best to ask her to leave the airline for good as she was the problem. You see the people in the room were smart and genuinely kind-hearted, they thought their way to this result as it was the default mode that was set in play. What will the world think? If we don't show the crew that this is serious enough to lose your job they will not care about this? What we do here will show our corporate maturity to the regulatory board? They will think we are too lenient! The biryani element comes in with the thinking behind the decision. What will people think? What if I don't? What if I miss? But how will it seem to others?

By the time you reach sixty years old, you will probably realise no one ever cared as they were busy wondering about what others were thinking of them. It was around this point that I could smell this amazing biryani being served in the cafeteria! The thought crossed my mind, I'd rather have that biryani than this one right now.

I asked the question; if we recruited someone to replace this cabin crew was that new crew more likely to do the same thing? Or considering the massive blow this has given this crewmember, chances are zero that she would ever make this error again? Five minutes later she had kept her job and I was having that biryani instead of cooking one.

In our fear of being judged and covering all bases we enter this spiral of cooking a pot of biryani! You asked for white rice at an Indian restaurant and what you got in return was a biryani! For those of you who are good at history, give it a think – try to spot the biryanis all over the place. Invasions, war, diplomatic spats in relationships that took years to build, trade wars, how did people make something so simple into something so complicated?

Most important of all, how do we make life simple again?

Questions

- ✈ Sit back and ask yourself, what biryanis have you created?

- ✈ What could you have done differently at the time?

- ✈ Are you creating space to move freely in your life and decisions or restricting yourself with overthinking?

- ✈ What if you cared less what the world would think?

- ✈ What if you cared more about the good things some people think of you?

- ✈ Is anything permanent? If not, where does it go?

- ✈ How has complexity become an autopilot setting?

- ✈ Do you believe that without effort and hard work things don't get done?

- ✈ What in your life can only be done correctly by you and not entrusted to others?

- ✈ Think about your biggest problems in the past vs the small ones, which took the most out of you?

- ✈ What did you learn in solving the big problems?

- ✈ If you lost everything in your life, your job, home, relationships, how would you start over? What would be the first thing you would focus on?

- ✈ If disaster struck your home, what would you grab on the way out?

- ✈ Who in the world are you most important to?

- ✈ If you won so much money that you never had to work again, what would you make time for?

³ Attachment

> The root of suffering is attachment
>
> *Buddha*

I'm sure you may have read this before, though what does this really mean? Attachment to your Car? Rolex? Home? Relationships? Outcomes?

The famous Lao Tzu quote comes to mind, "If you realize that all things change, there is nothing you will try to hold onto".

The moment you attach yourself to anything, you have created a remote control for yourself and handed it over to the attachment. In the case of material things, I remember studying the Law of Diminishing Marginal Utility with my favourite economics teacher Mrs Maria Martins. She was an ace in economic studies and easily explained that when you acquire something today it has the highest value to you and as time goes by the value decreases. In this case, is attachment momentary? Does it reduce as time goes by? Does this hold the same with relationships? The longer you stay in the harder it is to get out?

One of the most common thinking errors that afflicts humans is the belief that it is better to chase an investment already made than to 'cut your losses'. This is one of the factors in a gambling addiction, because the gambler will continue to chase their losses rather than walk away. You only have to consider how opulent the average casino is to know who always wins. You might do the same with your car, continuing to pay for repairs rather than selling it and starting over. In relationships and jobs, you might think, "I've come this far, I'm sure it will start getting better soon". Your attachment to the work or time or money that you've already put in draws you in further.

Our journey to simplifying life and mastering the autopilot begins by recognising the attachments that are holding you back. Your attachments are neither good nor bad, useful nor useless. They are simply… attached. It's the attachment itself which causes you to stay where you are. You can't change career because you've invested so much in your current job. You can't leave a job you love to pursue your true calling because everything is nice for you right now. You can't leave a relationship which isn't serving you because the alternative could be worse. You can't leave a wonderful relationship to pursue you dreams because you don't want to risk losing something which is working just fine. You become attached to your past, bad or good, because the future is unknown.

And yet, all good things must come to an end. You know that you can either change the situation yourself or, if you wait long enough, it will change whether you like it or not.

In having fewer strings attached, life does get less complicated. Remember, impermanence is a permanent fact of life!

Let's begin to break attachment to the things in life which don't serve you.

The first step is to realise that you have no problem detaching from the things you don't want in your life. If you don't like the coffee from a particular cafe, you don't go there any more. If you don't like a TV show, you don't watch it. Think back ten years. What were the things you did, the places you went, that are no longer part of your life? What did you do with your spare time when you were younger? Whether you just lose interest in something or you actively avoid it, you can detach.

The hard part is learning to detach from the things you do like, the things you do want. Does this mean you have to give up your favourite things? No! It only means that you can be free of believing that you need these things. You can realise that you can choose or not choose these things.

Detachment takes practice, mainly because you don't even realise you're attached to something until it's taken away from you!

Acknowledgment

The biggest challenge in freeing yourself from attachment is to realise that you are attached! So the first thing to do is realise that you are attached right now, to everything in your life that you can't imagine living without.

One easy way to realise that you are attached to something in your life is to pay attention to the feelings you get when you think you will lose something. That feeling, which is fear, is telling you what you think will happen if something is taken away from you.

Think about what happens and how you feel when someone takes your parking spot, or sits in your seat, or reads your newspaper, or throws something away that you were keeping, or when your favourite brand or flavour isn't available, or when the weather changes and you have to cancel your plans, or when someone you expected to rely on isn't available for you.

You can imagine a child shouting, "It's not fair!" and the feeling is like the child inside you, shouting, wanting things to go back the way they were.

This feeling is not a good one, but it has a useful purpose - it's the early warning sign of attachment! Learn to recognise the feeling, take a breath, pause and think about what it is teaching to you.

Reflection

When you become aware of the feeling of attachment, the next step is to reflect on what it means to you. Concentrate on the feeling and think of times in your life that it reminds you of. This might take you back to your childhood, or your time at school, or maybe a boss you once had. When you start to realise the times when you felt like this, you can identify the pattern that causes the feeling. The feeling is normal. When you're a child, when you're facing an angry boss, the feeling is totally normal. When the cafe ran out of your favourite coffee, it's not normal. Well, it might be normal but it definitely isn't helpful! When you understand where this feeling comes from, you can begin to master it.

Acceptance

People who have high pressure and high status jobs had to work hard for their success, and they probably started working hard in school, and many times this is fuelled by a feeling that what they do is never good enough, they can always try harder or achieve more. So the normal thing to do when life doesn't go your way is to beat yourself up. This is your autopilot working for you. When your autopilot is keeping you on course and life is going to plan, you don't notice it working. Suddenly, when external forces push you off track, your autopilot kicks in and you can feel the resistance! So the important thing to do here is to realise that you're not doing anything wrong, and your autopilot is doing exactly what you asked it to do. And now it's time to change the settings and ask it to do something different.

Do you think the autopilot feels bad when the aircraft drifts off course because of a cross wind? Do you think the autopilot sits there at night and reviews its mistakes? Do you think that it beats itself up for not working hard enough?

The autopilot gets information from the sensors around the aircraft. When it detects a difference, a deviation, it simply, quietly corrects the deviation or informs the pilot. No fuss, no sighs, no bad mood. Its job IS to correct. When the aircraft is on course, the autopilot is idle! There is no deviation from the programmed settings, so nothing for the autopilot to do. You could switch it off and nothing would happen - for a short time!

You think that you're doing OK when life is going your way, and you beat yourself up when you're off course. You should be switching your thinking round! When life is OK, you're cruising, your autopilot is doing nothing because there's nothing for it to do. You're playing safe, staying in your comfort zone. When life is heading off course, you're noticing! You're aware that you need to make a correction! This is good - this is normal. It's what your autopilot was designed to do. So, embrace these feelings and realise that you have an opportunity to make a course correction.

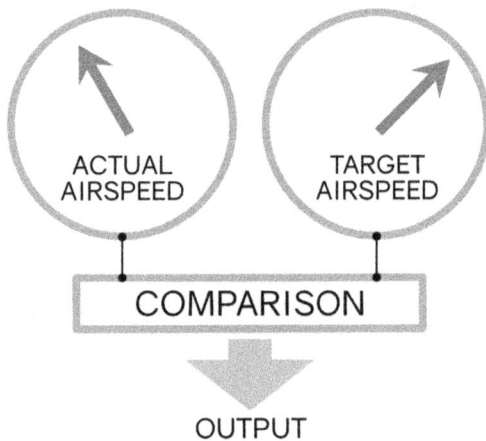

ACTUAL
AIRSPEED

TARGET
AIRSPEED

COMPARISON

OUTPUT

Reset

Your autopilot, just like the autopilot in an aircraft, is a self-correcting system with three parts; a target reference, feedback and an output that can be adjusted.

When a modern self-correcting system fails, it is designed to 'fail safe', in other words its output is set to a default position if the system fails. Think about a simple system like the cruise control in your car. Its output is to inform the engine management computer to accelerate or decelerate. If the road speed sensor fails, what do you want it to do? Assume that you want to go faster? No! You want its fail safe position to be 'off' so that the driver can take control.

You have a target state - your life goals, your self-image and so on. You have feedback systems - your senses. You have a comparison computer - your mind. Most of what your system is doing is totally outside of your awareness. You pick up your coffee, test it, too hot, blow on it, drink it carefully, swallow, all without a moment's thought. Have you always had your coffee the same way? Did you once take cream, and now you take it black? Do you have more or less sugar than you used to? Stronger? Weaker? Different blend? Your autopilot always tests for the 'right' coffee, and the 'right' coffee has changed over time. So, the autopilot, the habit system in your brain's basal ganglia doesn't care what you want, it just gets it for you! It doesn't tell you you're drinking too much coffee, it just checks the coffee against your current target state. Your neocortex, your rational, thinking brain, the part of your brain that is aware of these words right now has the ability to reset the target state. Your autopilot then achieves that state for you.

Think about your fail safe position, your default mode. What do you do when you don't know what to do? Is that what you really want? And how can you reset your autopilot to take you where you really want to go?

Freedom

When you've reset your autopilot once, you must learn the most valuable lesson of all - that you can reset it any time you like! You can change your mind. You can go in a different direction. You can have your coffee black with 6 sugars, or white with none, or you can switch to green tea. Sure, other people will say, "Hey, don't you drink coffee?" because you have to remember that you are part of their autopilot! You're part of their world, their feedback, their expectations! They want you to stay the same, they don't like it when their world changes without their permission!

So you can answer their question in the spirit of true freedom from attachment: "I used to. I changed my mind."

Questions

- ✈ What can you not live without?

- ✈ How and who would you be without that?

- ✈ What are some of the situations you try to influence?

- ✈ What expectations do you have from people who you are attached to?

- ✈ What expectations do you have of people who you are attached to?

- ✈ What do you do when you don't know what to do?

- ✈ What have you changed your mind about in the past?

- ✈ What are you ready to change your mind about now?

- ✈ What have you already changed your mind about, but you're afraid to tell anyone?

- ✈ If you let go of attachment, where would you land?

- ✈ What are the best attachments in your life, the ones that define you?

- ✈ How might those attachments change if you were to redefine yourself?

- ✈ Who or what is attached to you or depends on you?

- ✈ If you were no longer here, what would happen to those attachments?

- ✈ Without those attachments, would you still be here?

- ✈ Without those attachments, what motivates you?

- ✈ Without attachments, what are you free from?

- ✈ Without attachments, what are you free to do or be?

⁴Expectation

> Peace begins where expectations end
>
> *Buddha*

The autopilot mode is to expect, and this habit of expectation is engrained into us from a young age. Your brain is constantly trying to make predictions about the future, and this makes your expectations hard to shake off.

Expectation takes a few forms:

- ✈ What you expect from others
- ✈ What others expect of you
- ✈ What you expect from yourself
- ✈ What other expect from themselves
- ✈ Expectations of life

The goal from an autopilot perspective is to notice when your autopilot is set to expectation mode, when your autopilot setting is working against you instead of for you. Notice when you release the switch and let go of expectations, what happens? Peace transcends and life gets more flexible. Expectation is a loop, a habit, and every habit can create another.

You could think of an expectation as an attachment - to the future. The most obvious thing that we can say about the future is that it doesn't actually exist. It is not real. Only the present is real. The past is a memory and a set of clues, evidence that remind us, and the future is a complete fabrication. You can talk all you like about what you're going to do tomorrow, but there are no guarantees until tomorrow is today, and today becomes yesterday. As for seeing the results of your actions, they're a long way off!

We create expectations of ourselves and of other people. We expect other people to behave in certain ways, to understand our needs and our instructions. We expect the physical world to obey the laws of nature, but human beings have free will. In fact, if we think about our autopilot, most accidents today are not caused by the machine, they are caused by the human second guessing the machine.

Errors are caused by the system in which the human operates; complexity, threats, errors, miscalculations, poor design, inadequate resources, environmental conditions and procedural issues all come together to bring in failure. The human system is quite similar, with multiple influences that effect the way we manage our own system, including habits, fears, distractions, beliefs and behaviours. When something new shows up, it is easy to start second guessing. That's fear, because your predictions are no more than wild guesses and the outcome has no guarantees. Your brain will always protect you from losses!

When we have expectations of people, it creates that biryani! We start second guessing and trying to make allowances for things that other people haven't even done yet! We try to guess and anticipate every possible reaction and get tied up in knots. And no matter how much we try to plan ahead, other people still react in unexpected ways!

We want people to operate from our model and navigate our map of the world. Expectation is interlinked with attachment, when we expect, we are attached to the outcome. We have numerous expectations every single day.

- ✈ You expect the floor to be there when you get out of bed in the morning
- ✈ You expect your coffee to be just the way you like it
- ✈ You expect other people to respond to you in the same way that they did yesterday

Expectation is a great measurement tool and also the root cause of bias! When we expect, we have something in mind to measure against, in airline crew training we emphasise on having a healthy expectation for things going wrong. Most procedures are built into the aviation system expecting the failure scenario. On the other hand, when we have a strong expectation for things to play out a certain way, we enter the confirmation bias lounge. We set ourselves up to expect "A", we do everything to seek information to confirm "A" despite "B" staring in our face. Not your fault, remember error is part of the human condition. The point here is, expectation has its place within certain systems and events in life. As a matter of fact expectation is the key element in manifestation! (Desire – Dedication – Trust – Expect).

What do we do? Expect the best or the worst? Is it good to expect or bad? Should we let go of all expectation? What would we ever achieve if we didn't expect things to go well?

By no means am I advocating that you kill all your dreams and expect nothing. Expecting nothing is not the same as being open to expecting anything.

Expectation without adaptability is where things get complicated. It can also tie you up in knots, when you can't adapt to a situation that does not meet your expectation. When we have high expectations of others or situations it's usually from our own issues attached to perfectionism and negative beliefs - If I'm not X I cannot get Y. High expectation is the fuel for anger, stress and depression, to name a few. Your expectations are one element only, what about what others expect from you? In corporations, these are often well defined with Key Performance Indicators and specific Job Descriptions. In relationships, you surely need to have certain expectations from each other to nurture the bond, be it that of life partners, friends, siblings, parents or children. Your expectations come from your own experiences and from seeing other people's mistakes. Setting agreeable expectations is the way to go, defining boundaries and having these maintained through mutual trust and good communication.

Here's how you can simplify your expectations:

- ✈ Keep it simple, choose what you expect carefully
- ✈ Under expect and over ask
- ✈ Remember that in expecting there are no guarantees
- ✈ Dream big and ask for more
- ✈ Expect the unexpected
- ✈ Let other people help you

Resilience is key to aligning your behaviour if things don't turn out the way you expect. Resilience isn't about resisting when life doesn't go your way, it's about being flexible and bouncing back more easily. Things, people, situations and events unfold every minute that can influence your outcomes. Most importantly, be kind to yourself, we set expectations for ourselves quite high and beat ourselves up over not fulfilling them. Ask yourself how you can make this easy, simple and brief, with the least possible stress, the least required amount of effort and with the greatest amount of love for yourself.

We might set expectations for ourselves quite high and beat ourselves up for not fulfilling them. Instead of bouncing back, the focus may turn to self-assessment and self-critique. This is essential for learning and feedback, but if you're locked into this mode it will only sabotage you instead of enabling you to upgrade your game.

Set your mode to; encourage, advance, promote, elevate, upgrade, and develop. You're not a failure. You're not a success. You're a learner.

Questions

- When you were a child, how did you imagine your future would look?

- When you were a child, what were the aspects of your life which you assumed would always be the same?

- What do you feel the future holds for you?

- What makes you certain that you have a future?

- For you to be successful, what do you expect other people to do?

- Do you expect other people to do something for you, with you or to you?

- What would it be like to live without expectation?

- Is your future expectation based on your past experience?

- Which experiences have you chosen to base your future on?

- How could you base your future on a different set of past experiences?

- What if the stories you tell about your past are not true, they are simply one version of events?

- How would changing your stories change your expectations?

- What will happen next in your life?

- What are you prepared to do to get the life you truly deserve?

5 Thoughts & Beliefs

Your beliefs become your thoughts,
Your thoughts become your words,
Your words become your actions,
Your actions become your habits,
Your habits become your values,
Your values become your destiny

Gandhi

What you believe is what locks you in for the better or for the worse. Your life is determined by what you believe. If you believe it, you will live it, if you don't it holds no value and control over your life.

How do you even know what you believe? You know certain truths about the world you live in. You accept those truths as absolute, and you expect other people to know them too, so much so that you are genuinely surprised when people disagree.

Maybe you have seen the rise of 'Flat Earthers' over the last few years. Have you tried to argue with one? Have you tried to convince them of your truth? If you have, you'll know how futile this is, and it is equally futile for them to convince you of their beliefs. This example is confusing because, surely, everybody knows that the Earth is round. From an aircraft, on a good day, you can even see the curvature of the horizon. They would say that this is an optical illusion. It's exhausting to argue!

So consider this. How do you know the Earth is round? Have you seen it with your own eyes? Or were you told in school? You've seen photos. Faked! You've heard stories from astronauts. Actors! Beneath the Flat Earth argument, there is a deeper issue - don't believe the establishment, believe your own eyes. If you can't see it, touch it, feel it, then 'they' are lying to you. Why? To control you. The Flat Earth movement is resistance to control from Big Brother.

Every decision you make starts with a belief. We base our decisions on what we know to be true, what we believe. But just because you've always believed something doesn't mean you have to continue to believe it. You already changed your beliefs about many things in your life.

Stanford psychologist Lee Ross found that people tend to ignore the situation when they're looking at their behaviour. He called it the "fundamental attribution error" - our preference for blaming behaviour on "the way I am" instead of "the situation I'm in."

The first step, then, is to create new situations. Instead of creating an uphill battle for yourself every day, trying to change the decisions you already made, create a downhill slope and give yourself a push. Create an environment that makes change easy.

When you reduce the gap between what you say and what you do, tough decisions get easier. When you make difficult decisions without giving yourself time to think, you fall back into old thinking habits. You act out of belief, not analysis. Your autopilot has gone back to its default mode! So when you're under pressure, you'll react the same way you always do, and then afterwards you'll make up some story about how you did the right thing. You didn't do the right thing. You did the only thing you could do, and then you made up a story about how it turned out right.

What I love about our beliefs is how we fight for them. How many people were prepared to die for their beliefs? From terrorism to war to divorce to political parties? Friends for years walk their separate ways when one believed in today's popular political ideology and another believed the complete opposite. What beliefs are holding you trapped? In the aviation industry we believe in the reliability of standard operating procedures because they are tried and tested, they are risk assessed and they will stand up in court.

This is all good until a latent glitch turns it around and the belief that we swore by for the past decade is dismissed with a new replacement. The system is always changing. What was the cure for 'X' 10 years ago? Is it the same today? Be flexible in your views because your beliefs will determine the quality of your life. More importantly, it takes a long time for inconvenient evidence to finally get through the thick protective shell of your beliefs and create change.

Why is this?

Imagine you get home tomorrow and as you walk in through your front door, you notice that something has moved. Something small, maybe an ornament or a small piece of furniture. No-one else is at home. Why do you notice it? How do you feel? What thoughts cross your mind? What do you think has happened?

The next day, you get home and something else has moved. What new thoughts do you have?

The next day, you get home and as you open the door, carefully, the colour of the walls has changed. The furniture has changed. What's going on?

The feeling you get when you imagine this is insecurity. From a very early age, your brain started creating a map of the physical world that you live in. You know that game of peek-a-boo that you can play with babies? You know how they never stop laughing at the surprise of you suddenly reappearing? And maybe you discover that day when the game stops being funny. You hide and the child knows to look for you. What happened? Simply, their brain developed to the point where it created a map of the world, and that map exists whether they can see the world or not. Up until that point, if they can't see it, it doesn't exist.

The newborn baby lives only in the present moment. The child lives in the world where they know the cookie jar is hidden on the top shelf, they know where their toys are when they run in from school, they know what to say to their parents to get some extra treats or extra time before bed.

Your sense of 'psychological safety' is based entirely on this map that your brain creates. Every life experience you have gets stored away as a point on the map. Your brain then uses the map to navigate through the world. You know where things are in your home. You can drink your coffee without having to look at it. You can drive to work without having to think about where you're going. And sometimes, you drive to the store and end up heading towards work.

Your mental map is a critical resource for your autopilot, without it you have no way of knowing how to get to where you want to be, not only physically but also in terms of your goals and achievements. Your map contains the steps you need to take to get what you want in life, learned by carefully watching people around you to see which behaviours get praise, which get punishment, which get attention and which get promotions. This map is where your beliefs are stored!

Listen to what to argue for, that's your autopilot setting, the mode that you're locked in. How far will you fight to keep hold of your beliefs? Your safety in the world depends on it! But by holding on to it, what are you preserving?

Questions

✈ What are you thinking, right now?

✈ Are you in control of your thoughts?

✈ If you are now thinking about an elephant, where did that idea come from?

✈ How do you know what you believe in?

✈ Think of a belief which other people have which you do not share. How do you defend your own beliefs?

✈ The news agencies and media show political bias, based on what beliefs?

✈ How do you seek out information which reinforces your own beliefs?

✈ How do you reject advertising and news stories which contradict your beliefs?

✈ Do you even know where you inherited your political and social beliefs from?

✈ How do you react when you're proven wrong?

✈ What life experiences have created your strongest beliefs?

✈ What beliefs are you prepared to change?

✈ What beliefs will you never change?

✈ What makes you believe that there are beliefs you will never change?

✈ What would have to happen in your life for all of your beliefs to change?

6

Resistance & Control

> Change is never painful, only the
> resistance to change is painful
>
> *Buddha*

For an aircraft to stay on course, it has to resist the world's attempts to push it in a different direction. The weather conspires to nudge the aircraft from side to side, up, down, faster, slower. So the job of the autopilot is to resist by controlling the various systems of the aircraft to maintain its focus on its target, even when the world is throwing many distractions at it. Even the maps app in your phone can receive data about the real time traffic conditions and reroute you around accidents and traffic jams.

When you think about your personal, built in autopilot, you will resist any attempts to push you off course, and you will try to exert more control to correct for changing conditions.

Resistance to change is normal because, remember, your psychological safety is based on the world being exactly the way that it was the last time you looked. However, if you keep trying to convince yourself that the world should fit your expectations, that resistance becomes stress, and it's stress that damages all systems. Stress is the result of opposing forces. Whether it's a bolt in an aircraft's wing, or a bridge carrying traffic across a river, or the mind-body system of a human being, stress is destructive. When we ask a system to do something that it was never designed to do, we can expect something to fail.

When you experience change, and you resist that change, your need to control increases because your autopilot is trying to restore the world to the way it should be - according to your own map.

I have a close friend who moved to a new country around 20 years ago. When I ask her if she plans on going back 'home', she says that it would be the end of her life! Its interesting that the resistance to that change is already set – the belief is already formed, the thought of it will set a domino of emotions rolling for her. I asked her what would happen if her husband felt it was time they moved back to their home country, she was lost for words. The idea was, literally, unthinkable.

The theme of this book is now coming alive for you, I hope. Change is from the inside out. Our default autopilot settings of the rules we live by are protecting us and also limiting us in ways more than we can imagine. Your autopilot is keeping your world exactly the way that it was yesterday, and it's stopping you from changing it for tomorrow.

If an aircraft is flying in a straight line, in good weather, what does the autopilot actually need to do? Newton's first law of motion says that the aircraft will continue in a straight line unless an external force pushes it off course. In good flying conditions, the autopilot is doing very little work, and you might not notice it doing anything at all. But what happens when the aircraft flies into an area of strong side winds, or warm air rising? Now the autopilot jumps into action, trying to correct for the forces pushing the aircraft off course. The autopilot is working hardest when the outside environment is creating the greatest resistance to what the pilot intends.

When your life is running exactly the way you want, you don't notice. Your autopilot is working in the background, keeping you on course. It's only when you run into problems that you suddenly notice resistance, and that's when your first action is to try to control.

What are the things you do to increase your control?

- ✈ Shut off outside communication

- ✈ Use more force

- ✈ Speak louder

- ✈ Try to convince others of your truth

- ✈ Do what you want and hide it from others

The main problem with control is that it's an illusion! Your brain is playing tricks on you. Just like in the aircraft cockpit, when the pilot operates the controls, there are no cables connecting to the control surfaces on the wings. What the pilot is really doing is asking for the computer's help to move the aircraft, and then the computer has to decide if that seems like a good idea. You've heard of many cases where the pilot and the computer disagreed, and the computer won the argument because it was really the one in control. Normally, this increases safety but sometimes the opposite happens, usually when the pilot is asking the aircraft to do something that it wasn't designed to do!

Even in your own mind, your autopilot is in control and your conscious, thinking mind is simply along for the ride, occasionally asking if the autopilot could change direction. Neuroscience research has shown that the time lag between an action and the thought that leads to the action is around half a second. What might surprise you is that the action comes first. Yes, you read that right! Your body moves, and around half a second later, your conscious mind makes up a story about how you meant to do it. By creating the illusion of control, your autopilot lets you feel safe while also allowing it to get on with its job.

So why have a conscious mind at all?

Think of it this way - your conscious mind is great for solving puzzles, planning ahead, weighing up complex decisions. Your autopilot is great for reacting in the moment. What a perfect combination!

The problem, and the resistance, comes when the two start to compete with each other.

Questions

✈ What do you do when you don't get your own way?

✈ And what do you *really* do when you don't get your own way?

✈ When life feels 'difficult', what are you resisting?

✈ How do you control?

✈ How do you resist being controlled by others?

✈ Where do you feel most in control?

✈ What happens when you lose control?

✈ What do you do to intentionally lose control?

✈ What needs to happen for you to let go of what is controlling you?

✈ What would happen if you controlled less and observed more?

✈ How does controlling protect you or others?

✈ Can control be delegated? Redistributed? Or does your control have to control you?

✈ When do you realise that you are being controlled by your need to control?

✈ How are you attached to control?

7

Judgement & Dependency

> If you need encouragement, praise, pats
> on the back from everybody then you
> make everybody your judge
>
> *Fritz Perls*

Think about the day you decided to follow your current career path. Think back to what, or who inspired you. Think about where the idea came from. There was a time when you didn't even know that this career existed, and then one day, you saw something, heard something, and that was it! Your autopilot was locked and now, here you are today.

While you're remembering the inspiration for your career choices, consider this: Who were you trying to please or impress with your career choice? Whose approval and praise were you trying to win? And whose approval was withheld just enough to keep pushing you along that same path? Today, what continues to motivate you?

Don't worry, seeking approval isn't a problem! We're social animals, we depend on being part of a group. A family, a team, a crew. No one person can do everything alone. We achieve more when we work together, pooling resources and sharing skills and knowledge. When a team achieves great things, it's because each person knows how they contribute and each person can contribute something different yet contribute equally. A high performing team recognises that the overall task wouldn't be achieved without every single person in the team doing whatever they do best.

The problem is when you begin to think that you can't survive without that approval, when you think that you depend on it. The problem starts when approval is the only reason you do something.

You have heard of the idea of a 'mid life crisis', when a person has lost sight of why they're doing what they do in life. They have a high paying job and a big house and a nice car... and they can't remember why any of it is important. One of the reasons why people get to this point is that they start out on a career path chosen to impress other people, maybe their parents, teachers or friends. They love to hear their parents brag about their successful children. They push themselves harder and harder in the hope of one day hearing those precious words… "Well done, I'm proud of you"

If those words never come, this person becomes more and more detached, emotionally, from the life they have created. Their life feels like an illusion, a facade. And one day, they run away from it all, join a spiritual retreat in the mountains, file for divorce, buy a sports car, gamble away their savings, take up dangerous sports, all to feel alive again, all to look in the mirror and see the person they remember once being.

Wouldn't it be better, and less expensive, simply to follow the life path that you choose for yourself from day one?

But life and society isn't like that. We glamourise certain jobs, advertising and glossy magazines push us down a path. We see what other people have got and we want it. And we become dependent on the things we bought and the habits and expectations we created!

Dependency creates a fragile bridge between you and the people you depend on. Countries fought for decades to gain independence. Why? What did they think was on the other side of dependency? When a country doesn't have a certain resource in abundance and is reliant or dependent on another, what do you notice? There is an unfair advantage and a top down imbalance in the relationship. Countries tend not to fight for independence once, they have revolutions and coups over and over again. The military overthrows the monarchy, the democracy overthrows the military, the people overthrow the military, the monarchy rises from the people. History keeps repeating itself! So maybe the problem isn't independence, maybe the problem is human nature, the need for equity and the tendency to see inequity. We're back to the child's complaint; "It's not fair!"

Dependency is a vicious game too, the more you make people dependent on you the more control you think you have. How many dependency trainers have you met? Yes, people train you to be dependent knowingly, but more so unknowingly. People withhold information or resources. They say, "Let me do that for you", or, "I have what you need, let me get some for you". And when you begin to rely on what they give you or do for you, you're hooked.

A coach of mine once taught me that people will remain in a relationship in the way you trained them at the start of the relationship.

The more you pile up on yourself to ease the load on someone else, the more you are training dependency. I have worked with people in unhappy relationships who won't get out. What they are dependent on in the relationship is more important than their happiness!

If you are dependent on others, be it your parents or friends, siblings or society, to validate your self-worth, your autopilot needs to disengage here. Yes, this needs work at a deeper level too, I have a friend whose dad was her biggest critic, this fuelled her drive to strive, it also left him in control of her self-worth. What served her as a child to persevere was failing her as an adult in other areas of her life. Dad moved on and the validation she was looking for needed a new leader. Is this bad though? Otherwise the autopilot is programming itself, and that's not a good thing either. So in this case, that external validation isn't a bad thing but it's like the role of a critic for an artist or writer. Critical feedback can lead to the artist withdrawing, hiding and hating the world. Critical feedback can also help the artist to see what they're not seeing, helping them to take away what is unnecessary and refine their craft. The artist is too close to their work and can no longer tell what is good and what isn't, and an external point of view is valuable. The artist who rejects criticism isn't seeking growth, they are seeking approval. They're not really asking, "What do you think?", they're saying, "Tell me that you love it!"

What are your memories of school? Maybe the building? The teachers? The ones you hated and the ones you loved? Maybe the exams. Do you remember how you felt about your exam results? Were your parents always proud that you had tried your best? Or did they have high expectations for you? Did they push you to work harder? And how has that affected you now? Do you still carry that dependency on your achievements?

Humans are social beings; we like to please and share with others. But can our need for approval be harmful?

Yes, it certainly can! It's one of the causes of emotional dependence. Do you need to please everyone, or only those who are really important to you? Who are those important people? Do they have to approve of everything you do? Do you approve of everything they do?

It's one thing to know what you want to do and what you want your loved ones to approve of. It is another thing entirely to feel like something isn't worth doing if others don't approve of it. You are acting out of a desire to win approval, not because the action itself is right for you.

Barbara De Angelis puts it like this; "If you aren't good at loving yourself, you will have a difficult time loving anyone, since you'll resent the time and energy you give another person that you aren't even giving to yourself."

Emotionally dependent people need the affection, attention, and the approval of others to an unhealthy degree. They have an irrational fear of loneliness and abandonment, which makes them more submissive in their interpersonal relationships. This means they are more likely to behave in a way that pleases those around them, while failing to please themselves. These people then long for protection and affection so intensely that they completely lose themselves in the relationship. As a result they maintain that relationship, regardless of the actual quality of the relationship. They establish intense and unstable bonds, in place of healthier ones.

Emotional dependence impacts our psychological wellbeing. The problem with depending too much on others emotionally is that if the person doesn't receive the disproportionate attention and affection that they require, they start to irrationally doubt their own worth and how much others appreciate them. This has a negative influence on their emotions and self-esteem, they then start to feel rejected, denied, and abandoned. The resulting sadness is overly intense, which can lead to a vicious cycle of emotional emptiness and dissatisfaction, often culminating in depression.

The only person you're going to spend your whole life with is yourself. Therefore, your well-being should not depend on the approval of others, but on the approval of yourself. This means that the first person you should try to please with your actions is yourself.

But what can you do to love yourself more? One simple exercise is to do something every day that makes you feel good, both physically and psychologically. It will take some effort at first since most of us aren't used to prioritising self-care and self-love. However, over time you'll start to develop more positive feelings towards yourself. By doing this, you'll prevent yourself from falling victim to emotional dependence.

You would encourage, support and cheer on your best friend, sibling or even a stranger. Start with you.

Questions

- ✈ What is your greatest failure in life?
- ✈ What is your greatest success?
- ✈ Who told you the difference between failure and success?
- ✈ What did you show your parents?
- ✈ Did you get the reaction you hoped for?
- ✈ What is the one thing that you always wanted your parents to say to you?
- ✈ What would happen if you said that to yourself?
- ✈ What would happen if you said it to other people?
- ✈ How are you cheering yourself on through your day?
- ✈ What role do you play in your dependency on others?
- ✈ Who are you dependent on and for what?
- ✈ What do people depend on you for, and how does that make you feel?
- ✈ When you depend on yourself to validate your self-worth, how does that feel?

{}^{8}Perfection &
Procrastination

A man who procrastinates in his
choosing will inevitably have his choice
made for him by circumstance

Hunter S Thompson

Perfectionism is defined as "a combination of
excessively high personal standards and overly critical
self-evaluations." Perfectionism can severely impact
our mental and physical health. Anxiety and
depression are some of the mental health problems
that mental health practitioners have repeatedly linked
with perfectionism.

One study, for example, found that over half of
people who died by suicide were described by their

loved ones as "perfectionists." Another study found that more than 70 percent of young people who died by suicide were in the habit of creating "exceedingly high" expectations of themselves. This demonstrates that toxic perfectionism seems to hit young people particularly hard. According to recent estimates, almost 30 percent of undergraduate students experience symptoms of depression, and perfectionism has been widely associated with these symptoms.

However, the negative impact of perfectionism does not stop at mental health. Some studies have found that high blood pressure is more prevalent among perfectionistic people, and other researchers have even linked the trait with cardiovascular disease.

Additionally, when faced with physical illness, perfectionists have a harder time coping. One study found that the trait predicts early death among those who have diabetes, and research conducted by Prof. Flett and his colleagues found that people with Crohn's disease, ulcerative colitis, or who have had a heart attack have a much harder time recovering. As Prof. Flett writes, "A link between perfectionism and serious illness is not surprising given that unrelenting perfectionism can be a recipe for chronic stress."

So, how do we counter the harms of perfectionism?

Self-compassion, the practice of self-kindness consistently helps to reduces the strength of the relationship between perfectionism and depression for both adolescents and adults. It might also be helpful to simply take a moment and acknowledge the fact that whatever goals you set yourself out to achieve in life, it will be difficult. By acknowledging the difficulty in achieving what you want, you are giving yourself the capacity to make mistakes, and then learn from those mistakes. Rather than berating yourself for missing the mark of perfectionism, which as we have seem does far more harm than good. What does the word 'mistake' even mean? It means an error, a deviation. Remember, your autopilot cannot keep you on course if there is no deviation to correct. The word comes from miss take. Think about a 'take' in the sense of the movie industry. How many takes are needed for the director to tell the story they imagine? Is the whole scene, the whole movie recorded in a single take? Of course not. Do actors sometimes 'get it wrong'? Well, yes, but then many modern movies are edited to incorporate those miss-takes, to give the movie a more natural, human, spontaneous feel. Sometimes, a scene will be unscripted and the actors will be encouraged to improvise, and only during the editing process does the director decide which take worked the best. So in that sense, a mistake isn't a failure, it's an opportunity to deviate, to improvise, to create, even to learn.

A while back I decided not to be perfect, today it's the one thing I have perfected, perfectly!

Perfection is a killer, but hang on! What about attention to detail? Doesn't the creation of a masterpiece painting or sculpture require perfection? What about that true passion for the work you do, knowing its perfect? When the pilot lands the plane, is a rough estimate good enough? Are the passengers happy if the pilot gets near the runway?

As an interviewer, one of the questions that came up in an assessment questionnaire was, "You have been assigned a project with a deadline, one day before the deadline it is almost complete but not perfect. Would you delay it and seek an extension to perfect it or release it and work it through whilst launched?"

The correct answer? – Release it. But why? Why not wait just a little longer and get the perfect version? Because perfection is subjective and an illusion! The system is not supposed to stop to get perfection, it is meant to move. Perfecting is a process, not an endpoint. Think about the computer you use. What was the first version? When perfection comes in technically they should have never released the oldest edition and they should still be perfecting the one you are working on. Microsoft should have waited until today to launch Windows. Who needed 3.1, or 95, 2000, XP…? None of them were perfect.

Perfection is the enemy of progress and, yes, it can fuel procrastination. Perfection is a killer and it consumes an unbelievable amount of energy. Procrastination is a stress management strategy. You procrastinate because of a fear of taking action. People tell you to stop procrastinating, like it's a switch that you can turn on or off. The fact is, there is an underlying foundation for procrastination. Until you stop to examine that, your autopilot is stuck in the wrong mode.

There's a simple system for dealing with procrastination, called the Five Minute Rule.

When you procrastinate, your brain is overwhelmed by the size of the task in front of you. This is an illusion - the size of the task is the size you're imagining. If I asked you to build a new airport, where would you start? How would you design it? What colour would the light switches be in the back offices? What type of glass in the windows? How many power points in the staff kitchen? Can you even imagine the scale of such an enormous task? Of course not. Project managers report to program managers who report to program directors who report to commercial directors... and any one person is only responsible for one tiny part of the project, the part that one person can 'get their head around'. Huge, challenging tasks aren't completed in one session. They're broken down into simple, understandable, manageable steps.

The Five Minute Rule works like this. You take a task that you have been putting off and you commit to doing only five minutes of work on it. At the end of the five minutes, you stop. If you want to stop earlier, you keep going. If you want to keep going, you stop. At the end of those five minutes, you review your progress and see how the task looks different. Now you can stop, or you can continue. If you choose to stop, that's not a failure, that's a choice to continue another day. Five minutes is enough to change your perspective, make a start and break the task down.

To paraphrase Erma Bombeck, procrastination is like a rocking chair, you're busy doing something, but it never gets you anywhere.

Deecide not tu be perfeckt.

Questions

✈ In which areas of your life are you a perfectionist?

✈ What do you do which is never quite good enough?

✈ What did you mean to do today but didn't?

✈ What did you do more than once today because the first attempt wasn't quite good enough?

✈ When you put more effort into a task than it needs, what are you afraid of?

✈ Has your worst perfectionist fear ever come true?

✈ What's the one thing you have been avoiding?

✈ What would happen if you achieved that one thing?

✈ What more would you achieve if you really put your mind to it?

✈ Who sets the standard for your job performance?

✈ Who set the standard for your performance as a human being?

✈ How are you failing to meet that standard?

✈ Are you a lenient or a tough critic of your own work?

✈ What if you were honest with yourself?

✈ What wonderful things have you achieved by trying too hard?

✈ What could the excess time and energy have been diverted to?

✈ When will you realise that you are perfect, right now, and yet tomorrow you can know more and be more?

^{9} Stress

> The greatest weapon against stress is our ability to choose one thought over another
>
> *William James*

Stress is defined simply as the result of opposing forces acting upon some object. The psychological sensation of stress is defined as 'a state of mental or emotional strain or tension resulting from adverse or demanding circumstances'.

Pressure is not the same as stress.

Pressure can cause you to respond, to take action. Pressure can get you moving. Think of an aircraft engine. The immense air pressure at the front causes no damage because that pressure enables the aircraft to move forwards as the incoming air is directed out of the exhaust. But what about pressure from two different directions at the same time?

Your body is trying to move in opposing directions, and this leads to both physical and mental stress which is damaging, even destructive.

Stress causes your body's cells to fail, and when they are replaced, the telomeres which protect your DNA are shortened, which leads to DNA copying errors which can become tumours. Stress can shorten your life by as much as 20 years. Compare this with an aircraft engine. Over the course of its life, all of its component parts might be replaced due to regular maintenance. Ideally, the worn parts are replaced with identical copies. What if we replaced those parts with used parts from other engines? Or what if we used cheap, substandard copies? The engine's life would be greatly reduced.

Some people say they need stress to be at their best. This just isn't true. Some people experience stress on a daily basis and so they get used to it, they actually become addicted to the stress hormones in their body. So they don't need stress, they're simply addicted to it!

The stress response has definite purpose and gets activated in the form of freeze, flight or fight, from the ancient reptilian part of your brain. There is no positive stress that comes out of this place. We are probably the only species on earth capable or worrying about something that hasn't happened yet, so we can even get stressed about a future that we are only imagining!

Stress begins as a conflict within your mind. Your mind is a simulator of reality, enabling you to make sense of what's going on around you, and also to make predictions about the future. When your future predictions are about something nice, we call that setting goals or daydreaming, and when your future predictions are about something bad, we call that worrying, and worrying can lead to stress if you don't do something to take action.

We get the same result with mechanical stress, such as the stresses which can damage an aircraft. Gravity is trying to pull the aircraft down, lift is trying to push it up. Modern aircraft are designed to be flexible to absorb these opposing forces. When passengers see the wings flexing up and down they can be terrified because they don't understand the advanced engineering principles and materials used! Even though the wings are flexible, they have limits, and the computer is programmed to stop the pilot from testing those limits. Sometimes, though, there are emergencies and extreme situations, so the engineers build in some leeway, some extra flexibility. The wing will survive, but once the aircraft is back on the ground, it has to be checked over, repaired, even scrapped because of the risk that the life span of the aircraft's structure has been reduced. Aircraft undergo regular checks for metal fatigue for exactly this reason. Many materials are flexible, but they don't last forever.

Your brain can create multiple simulations at the same time. You try to second guess what other people will do. What if they say this? What if they say that? Your brain, and so all of your simulated realities, are connected to your muscles, and your muscles act to make your imagined future real. When you're unable to act, or afraid to act, or you're experiencing conflict about how to act, the result is that you're trying to get your body into two or more conflicting states, which creates physical stress. So you make your own stress by imaging conflicting future situations!

Many illnesses are either directly caused by stress, or made worse by it, including:

- Hypertension – high blood pressure

- Asthma and allergic reactions

- Skin conditions such as psoriasis and eczema

- Obesity and eating disorders

- Greater susceptibility to colds and other virus

- Digestive issues such as IBS and stomach ulcers

You might say that you have a stressful job, but that can't be true. Look at some of the other people doing the same job as you. Some are more stressed, some are less. Some are having nervous breakdowns, some experience almost no stress at all. So clearly the job isn't stressful, it's your response to the demands of the job which creates stress.

So let's not assume that stress is guaranteed, let's look at some ways to reduce stress.

First of all, let's look at those opposing forces. What are the forces pushing or pulling you in different directions? When you think about where the stress is really coming from, right away you can see that it's at least partly based on what you're imaging is going to happen, not what is actually happening right now.

If you're stressed, whether by your job or something more personal, the first step to feeling better is to identify the cause. The worse thing to do is to redirect the stress into something else, to 'self medicate' with drinking, smoking or maybe something stronger. Some people divert stress into their personal relationships, causing even more damage. It's much better and easier to change the opposing forces rather than trying to reduce the stress after it has already built up.

Journaling

Journaling can be a very effective tool in managing stress and exploring and processing your emotions. The act of writing is important in two ways. First, it really helps to slow down your thought processes and put you back in control. Second it gives you a record that you can review to identify patterns that you can then change. Just take a few minutes at the start and end of your day to write down anything that comes to mind and then every week, take time to reflect and then write your summary into your journal too.

Be active

Taking exercise can help to release the energy stored up in your body, and it can give you important time to distance yourself from the causes of stress so that you can come up with new ideas and ways of looking at the situation. When you're stressed you maybe don't feel like you have the time for exercise, but it's important to make time.

Take control

You can't take control in every situation that doesn't go your way, but you can always focus on one thing that you can control, no matter how small. Feeling like there's at least one thing you can control helps you to focus your energy, and all action is a good step forwards.

Connect with people

Talking to your family and friends really does help. Don't talk to them about sports and movies to distract yourself, talk to them about what's on your mind. First, you get used to sharing your worries and hearing yourself talking out loud can be a great 'reality check'. Second, you get to hear them saying, "me too", so you realise it isn't just you.

Take time for yourself

A lot of your working life is spent round other people, and maybe there are times when you feel you have to be a certain way or make conversation when you don't feel like it. Make sure you take time for yourself too, maybe to do some things that you like to do for yourself. It's important to balance time with others with time by yourself.

Set goals

Setting goals doesn't mean wanting to climb Everest or beat the 100m world record. It just means that you have things to look forward to, and that gives you a sense of time and helps to give you perspective on your current situation. Put events in your diary or on a calendar. Plan for things you're looking forward to, things that give you a sense of personal progress.

Stay healthy

When you're stressed it's easy to reach for cigarettes, alcohol, sugar, caffeine or maybe something stronger. The chemicals in these products affect your body and your brain, that's why they're all global multi-billion dollar industries. The main problem with them isn't the short term effect that they have, it's the fact that your body filters them out as toxins and returns your body to normal levels. The more of these chemicals that you consume, the more you need because as fast as you're putting them into your system, your body is taking them out again. This is how addiction works! So avoid becoming dependent on these external props and enjoy them without feeling like you need them.

Help others

A lot of psychology research says that we have a built in reward system for helping other people, which makes sense for a social species like humans. If we feel good about working together and taking care of each other then that's good for the survival of the group. So helping someone else, or just doing something nice for someone, or even just saying something nice to someone gets a reaction which makes you feel good about yourself and reduces your stress. If you don't do this, or you avoid it, it's probably because you think other people are going to be selfish or ungrateful or just ignore you. You might hold a door open for someone and they just walk through without noticing you, so you feel like your help isn't appreciated and then it's easy to decide not to help anyone. So choose the people who you help, and show your appreciation when they help you.

Breathing Exercises (1 to 5 minutes)

Breathing exercise can work quickly and be used anywhere without drawing attention to yourself. Simply focus on your breathing, notice exactly where in your body you are breathing and notice the rate of your breathing. Then begin to count from one to five as you breathe in, and then from five back to one as you breathe out. Continue until you feel that your energy levels are back to normal.

Mini-meditation (3 to 10 minutes)

Regular meditation works extremely well as a stress reliever for many people, and this might last up to thirty minutes. You can also use the same principles to refocus and get back in control if you've only got a few minutes between tasks.

1. While standing or sitting, become aware of your feet on the floor. Close your eyes.

2. Take a deep breath in as you move your focus of attention across your body, noticing any tension in your muscles.

3. As you breathe in and out, breathe slowly and deeply, focusing your attention on each breath. Listen to the sound of your breath, notice the movement in your body.

4. As you notice ideas, thoughts, words or other distractions coming into your mind, gratefully acknowledge and thank each one and allow them to drift onwards again.

5. At the end of the meditation, open your eyes, notice your surroundings and compare how you feel to how you felt just a few minutes before. Repeat the process if you wish.

Progressive Muscle Relaxation (3 to 5 minutes)

PMR can help you to fully relax your body in just a few minutes, and release stress in the process as your focus moves away from stress and towards relaxation. Starting in your toes, tense your muscles in one foot, hold for a few seconds and then release, noticing the relaxation as you do this. Then switch to the other foot, then your ankles, then your knees, your hands, your arms and so on. Work your way slowly all the way up your body to your face, your eyebrows, your eyelids and let the tension evaporate as you reach the top of your head.

Take a walk (10 minutes)

The change of scenery and the physical movement involved in walking can quickly break a cycle of stress.

These stress management techniques become more effective over time, as your body and mind become used to relaxing as you practice them, and as you get better at recognising the early signs of stress and taking time to get back in control. Certain techniques, particularly exercise and meditation, are especially effective at creating changes that help you to become more resilient toward stress with practice over time. As your awareness increases, your tolerance seems to increase too because you are acting earlier and not waiting until the stress is out of control. Practising stress management techniques helps you to relieve any tension as you face it and be prepared for whatever comes your way.

Questions

✈ How do you feel stress?

✈ How do you release stress?

✈ What would life be like without stress?

✈ Have you convinced yourself that you need stress?

✈ What is the right amount of stress for you to feel at your best?

✈ Are you addicted to stress?

✈ In what ways to you invite stress?

✈ What do you imagine a stress-free life to be like?

✈ How can you turn stress to your advantage?

✈ What stress do you cause for others?

✈ How is stress affecting your health and wellbeing?

✈ What is under your control?

✈ What is not under your control?

✈ How can you let go more easily?

¹⁰ Circumstances & Interpretation

> Circumstances are beyond human control, but our conduct is in our own power.
>
> *Benjamin Disraeli*

You are never at the mercy of your circumstances; you are at the mercy of your interpretations!

Only you can let your circumstances rob you of the full richness and potential of your life.

Instead of thinking that you are a victim of circumstances and you can't change the things that happen to you, realise that you can choose interpretations that support you and take you to a place of wellbeing. You can program your autopilot to recognise new meanings and take new actions.

I know a family where the wife and mother of their four children has a terrible, life threatening illness. I asked the husband how he was doing in such a situation, and he said, "Mark, 1% of my life is very hard and the other 99% is better than anything."

How would you react in such a situation?

You are at the mercy of your own interpretation!

The way we talk to ourselves can be cruel and unjust. If someone else talked to us the way we talk to ourselves in our own heads, we'd hate them and wouldn't want to be near them. So why do we tell ourselves these things?

The secret to changing your interpretation is to set your autopilot to find something useful, something valuable in every situation. When you decide on your interpretation and then you live it out, that becomes the source of your happiness.

Destructive interpretations take an obvious negative toll on our confidence and self-worth. We have interpretations of things we say about ourselves. Often, it sounds like this:

"I'm not enough."

"Everything I do is wrong."

"I'm unlovable."

"If they knew the real me, they wouldn't like me."

Often, people with these interpretations can't even accept hearing kind words.

So, where do these destructive interpretations come from?

People create destructive interpretations in early life before cognitive filters have developed in their prefrontal cortex. Perhaps a critical parent or caretaker was emotionally or physically absent. The child doesn't understand why adults have to go to work or stay away from home, or why they're preoccupied or worried or stressed. The child learns that it doesn't get the love it needs and might even think that they did something wrong or that they are unlovable. As the child grows up, they live out that interpretation and they apply it as the default setting.

Without correction, this mindset becomes the child's adult life! Your entire neurology is based around the beliefs that you adapt and interpretations you accept— and you'll keep reinforcing these beliefs and interpretations over and over again... Unless you break the cycle!

The solution to breaking that cycle is that you choose an interpretation that serves you and your life. You will have to open up some serious parts of your brain and go in deep to clean it out. Think of it as a full system reboot, a turn off and on again.

This is not easy to do when you're in the middle of the circumstances that are triggering you. In that moment, there is only one reality, only one possible interpretation of events. Someone might say to you, "Look on the bright side!" and you would reply, "That's easy for you to say, you should try being in my place!"

Yes, it is easy to say, and it's easy for you to say too. You know that you do this to others when you think they're seeing a distorted reality. You tell people that they need to get things into proportion or see the situation as an opportunity. Again, easier said than done in the heat of the moment.

So how do you break this cycle?

To start with, instead of trying to see things differently when you're in the middle of the situation, take a step back. A pilot doesn't program the autopilot half way to the destination. Everything is set up before take-off, ready for when it's needed. To reprogram your autopilot, you have to make time to think about the situations which cause you to get stuck in a certain way of thinking. Be honest with yourself, you know the patterns. If it happened before, it will happen again. There's no use in hoping and praying that it will be different next time, it won't - unless you choose to make it different. Take a look in your diary. What events are coming up in the near future that you know will make you feel isolated, pessimistic, negative? Take time right now to think of other interpretations, don't wait until you're there and it's too late.

For example, let's say that you don't like going to social events. Too many people, too much small talk. When you stop and think about it, you might realise you're afraid of something - how people see you, what people think of you, that kind of thing. You might think that they won't like you. Instead of trying to tell yourself that you'll be fine, of course they like you, be honest with yourself. When you tell yourself that it will be OK, you know deep down you are lying to yourself. You know the truth. So, accept the truth. They won't like you. And then ask yourself, why is that? How do you behave? Do you hide in a corner, talk to very few people, show no interest at all in other people or their conversations? Well, if that's the case then of course they don't know you, so they don't like you. They don't dislike you either. They simply don't know you because you haven't put yourself in a position for them to get to know you and then get to like you. Do you like every stranger you meet? Of course not! You don't even know them!

At the heart of the fear that drives a negative interpretation is a truth. When you acknowledge that truth you gain power from it. Only then can you choose to do something different, and when you do something different you get a different result. Don't worry about getting it 'right' - remember what I told you about being perfect! Just find one thing, anything, that you can do differently.

1. Choose an event or situation in the near future that you know will make you feel negative in some way

2. Be honest with yourself and look for what you think is going to happen

3. Find the fear behind this imagined future scenario

4. Acknowledge the truth behind the fear

5. Look at what you're doing to make that true

6. Choose to do something different - anything!

Questions

✈ How would you describe your circumstances in life, right now?

✈ How would you describe your circumstances to your best friend?

✈ How would you describe your circumstances to your boss?

✈ How would you describe your circumstances to a stranger?

✈ Why are these different?

✈ What interpretations in your life serve you well?

✈ Which interpretations do not serve you?

✈ And how does this actually serve you? How do you gain from being negative?

✈ How would a positive interpretation give you more choice and freedom?

✈ What would you then do with that new freedom?

Faith & Fear

> Faith is the confidence of things hoped
> for and the assurance of things not seen
>
> *Hebrews 11:1*

When you are making any kind of change, you can experience fear. When you're taking a risk, doing something new, trying something new, saying something that you need to say, standing up to someone… fear is the normal reaction.

If an aircraft's autopilot was given emotions, fear would surely be top of the list. Once we give the autopilot its settings, we want it to stick to them. We don't want the autopilot in an aircraft to have second thoughts or start trying out alternative settings. You make the decision and you program the autopilot, and you expect it to carry out your instructions. If the autopilot was to deviate from those instructions, you might want it to feel fear. Throughout history, fear has been used to control people, so in the simple system of the autopilot, fear is the easiest and fastest way to get the system to avoid deviating from the program.

It turns out that the part of your brain that creates fear isn't much more complex than the aircraft's autopilot. Your modern, evolved brain creates complex emotions such as pride, excitement and joy. Your ancient, reactive brain where your habits are formed creates more basic emotions, and from a survival point of view, the most important is fear.

Fear is a normal survival instinct and in many situations in life, fear is absolutely the right emotion to drive your behaviour. When you're facing a potential attacker in a dark alley, or feeling the hot breath of a panther on your neck in the jungle, you want fear to trigger your instinctive response to freeze and hide, then to get out of there as quickly as possible, and as a last resort, turn round and fight.

You might be the kind of person who claims to never feel fear. It's likely that your reactions are so fast that you feel the adrenaline rushing through your body and interpret fear as something else such as anger or exhilaration. Recent research into human emotions suggests that we interpret the physical feelings based on the environment we're in. Fear on a cliff edge feels very different to fear on a roller-coaster because the environment is different. The real threat is pretending that you don't feel it.

Susan Jeffers, author of the well-known book 'Feel the Fear and Do It Anyway' talks about the five truths of fear.

FEAR TRUTH #1

The fear will never go away as long as you continue to grow!

FEAR TRUTH #2

The only way to get rid of the fear of doing something is to go out and... do it!

FEAR TRUTH #3

The only way to feel better about yourself is to go out and... do it!

FEAR TRUTH #4

Not only are you afraid when facing the unknown, so is everyone else!

FEAR TRUTH #5

Pushing through fear is less frightening than living with the bigger underlying fear that comes from a feeling of helplessness!

Fear only becomes a problem when your brain perceives a threat in a situation when your life is not in danger, such as the time when you're asking your boss for a pay rise or complaining in the restaurant that you got a biryani when you only asked for white rice. You've probably been in a situation like that when you're saying, "You should complain!", and the person you're with is saying, "I don't want to make a fuss." They are afraid of the conflict, and you don't understand their reluctance because you're not afraid of the conflict. Why not? Because you're not the one who is imagining it!

Fear in these everyday situations doesn't come from what is happening, it comes from what you imagine is going to happen, and in these situations it's almost impossible to stop feeling the fear once it's starter, so if someone tells you to 'just calm down', that often makes things worse. Instead, acknowledge the fear and then carry on with what you're doing. In short, you can feel the fear and do it anyway.

The basic message is, OK, what you're about to do is scary. Is that going to stop you from doing it?

There is of course another way. There is no need to be afraid in the first place, especially in situations where fear comes from an imagined future. Instead, it's more useful to focus on what is happening rather than what you imagine might happen. When you experience that feeling of fear, ask yourself, is it real? Is it happening right now? Then focus on what is really happening, right now. Then, ask yourself what you can do, what action you can take. Shift from reaction to real action.

Fear is, in most everyday cases, a belief about the future. You might realise that there is another word that we use for a belief about the future - faith.

You can have faith in an idea, a person, even a religious or spiritual movement. You can even have faith in yourself. Sometimes, faith in yourself can cross the line into over-confidence.

Roosevelt understood this when he said, "We have nothing to fear but fear itself." Fear has the power to paralyse you when we most need to act. Fear would make you retreat when you need to advance forward. When you make any kind of change, by choice or by force, a fear of the unknown can come up. People who irrationally fear change often feel that they have no control over their lives. This is because our lives are constantly changing! Those who fear change tend to live in the past as their phobia makes them unwilling to move, to progress or to change anything from their routine. This inability to change and develop can severely impact your professional and personal lives. What if your autopilot was stuck 'on' and you were unable to turn it 'off'? You might feel helpless, frustrated, even frightened. This is what it's like to fear change.

The fear of change is evolutionary in humans. Since the dawn of time, man has liked - and needed - routine. It makes us feel safe, in control. But the normal fear of change becomes a full-blown phobia when it is irrational, persistent, and intense!

Emotional distress caused by many life changes can trigger such a fear of change. A child who has experienced moving multiple times in short periods of time or the death of a family member or loved one might also have experienced changes in financial situations or lifestyle owing to these changes. This can lead them to resist change of any type even in adulthood.

However, change is unavoidable! We find ourselves forced to accept change at every point in life. There are a variety of ways we can learn to respond to and therefore manage fear of change, including the following ideas.

Name the fear

Sometimes when fear creeps up on us, the source of the fear isn't obvious. When you feel afraid, identify what it is you're afraid of. Name it. Write it down, if it helps. Say, "I'm afraid of _____."

Imagine your success

Humans have an amazing ability to influence our outcomes, simply by our imagination. Many people however, have a habit of imagining the worst. By doing this, we set ourselves up for failure. Set yourself up for success by imagining a successful outcome. Set yourself up for success, not failure! Visualize success in your mind—what it looks like, feels like, sounds like, smells like, and tastes like. Write it down in a simple, story form, with you as the main character. This is your life, take control!

Act out your new story

Using the success you imagined as a script, take your first steps. You may feel weak knees at first but keep going! Pause to rest and catch your breath if you need to. When you're ready, take a few more steps. But, set your feet firmly in the direction you want to go, committed to going forward. Allow the story to change as you move forward into your new adventure. The story won't unfold exactly as you imagined it. Accept this and you will be in control, not the fear you once felt!

Questions

- When you imagine the future, what scares you?
- What are you doing to make your fears come true?
- Why are you afraid of admitting what you are afraid of?
- What do you have faith in to carry you through?
- What can you always rely on?
- Who can you always rely on?
- Who can always rely on you?
- What situations reduce your faith?
- What in your life gives you faith in the future?
- What are you doing to make your dreams come true?

¹² Boundaries & Ownership

> The difference between successful people and really successful people is that really successful people say 'No' to almost everything
>
> *Warren Buffett*

You've worked so hard to take control of your autopilot and set it to maintain the right course for you. The risk you face now is that other people can walk right in and change the autopilot settings to suit them, if you allow them to.

The secret to protecting the life you are creating for yourself is in setting boundaries and taking ownership for what is under your control.

When you say 'yes' to someone else, are you saying 'no' to yourself? How often do you feel that you are compromising?

You might think that a compromise is a good alternative to an argument, in which everyone involved gives way a little in order to preserve the relationship. In fact, a compromise is an agreement where no-one gets what they want!

Professional negotiators look for ways to make the discussion bigger rather than dividing up resources. They look for ways to create more options instead of reducing those options into smaller pieces. Compromise is a last resort, to be avoided if at all possible.

Sometimes, when physical resources are involved, there is no alternative. Imagine that two passengers are given tickets for the same seat. There is only one seat and they can't both sit in it! How do they resolve their conflict? They have to go to the person in authority, the Captain of the aircraft, who makes a decision. Who is the decision maker in your life? You, of course!

You want to be respected, and nothing commands respect like self-respect. When you respect yourself, you show other people the right example. Think of the people who you respect, can you see how their self-respect shines through?

Respect means seeing someone as an equal, so how can you see yourself as an equal? By seeing yourself as equal to everyone else! It doesn't matter what someone's job title is, or how much money they have, or where they live - you are equal to them as a human being, and they are equal to you. Human rights apply to every human, it doesn't matter what your status or colour or religion or gender is.

When you see yourself as equal in value to anyone else, equal in your rights, then you must also be equal in the responsibilities which go with those rights. If you expect other people to follow certain rules then you have to follow those rules too. So respect is based on a simple foundation, that because we are all equal to each other, every transaction that we make must also be equal. When someone brings you coffee, you say "thank you", and that's a fair and equal exchange. What happens when you hold a door for someone and they walk through without a word or even a nod? You feel resentful! Who do they think they are? You imagine calling them all kinds of names. You imagine letting the door slam in their face. You have been treated unfairly. Your kindness was stolen from you because they didn't fulfil their part of the bargain.

Our personal boundaries aren't as obvious as a fence or a "no trespassing" sign. Personal boundaries are invisible - until someone pushes against them.

Imagine you call out to the person who you held the door for. "Hey! Aren't you going to say thank you?"

What happens next? Do they continue to ignore you? Do they turn round and hurl insults at you? Laugh in your face for being so stupid as to help a stranger?

Remember the Circumstances & Interpretation chapter! What if they turn round, embarrassed, and say, "Oh! I'm so sorry, I was miles away. Thank you!" And what would be different if that was the reason you imagined from the start?

Your resentment was based on your interpretation of their lack of gratitude, and your interpretation was based on your expectations, and they were based on your life experience, and all of that had programmed your autopilot to assume the worst about someone.

Remember, your personal boundaries are invisible to other people until they push against them. How you respond in that moment tells that person a lot about you. And if you really want people to stay clear of your personal boundaries then it's your responsibility to tell other people where to find them.

The same goes for your experience of others, of course. When you cross someone else's boundary, how do you want them to treat you? Do you want them to bite your head off? Push you back, aggressively? Or is a gentle reminder all you need?

Even though personal boundaries can be challenging to navigate, setting and communicating them is essential for your happiness, your health, your well-being, and even your safety.

Setting your boundaries and respecting the boundaries of others is based on something that you learned very early on in your life - that you are a separate being to those around you. Up to a certain age, you didn't know that you had a mind that was separate to others. You experienced the world only in real time, through your physical senses, and when you closed your eyes at night, that world ceased to exist.

After that age, you learned to have fantasies and day dreams, you learned to lie and you learned that other people have a different experience of life, different opinions, different tastes and different ways of handling things.

Your boundaries are the line between you and others. Is that a physical barrier? Yes, it can be! Your body, your personal space, even your home, your car, your desk at work. You claim these as your territory and you start to feel anxious or even angry when someone crosses into it.

In any relationship, when people understand and respect each other's territory, they can coexist peacefully and the relationship is productive and free from conflict. But as soon as someone takes something of yours without asking, or sits next to you on the train, or takes over a task that you always like to do, you start to feel like they're stepping on your toes. Boundaries aren't only separating you from others, your boundaries are connecting you too. When you agree with someone, you talk about having 'common ground', like a piece of territory that you are happy to share.

Clear boundaries allow you to make yourself a priority, in your work life or your personal life. That doesn't mean that someone else can't be your priority, like your partner or children, it just means that you don't need to put yourself last just to keep someone else happy.

Your boundaries can be flexible too, so that you can adapt as the situation changes and as your relationships change. If you meet someone and then move in together, maybe get married, you now have to figure out how to share the space. You don't need two of everything! So you go through your kitchen utensils, your books, your music collection, and you figure out how to merge your boundaries.

Being in a relationship doesn't mean that your boundaries have to be the same. You could like a certain type of food, your partner might hate it. You might like to go to bed early, they might be a night owl. Having respect for each other's boundaries means that you are OK with how they like to do things, and they are OK with how you like to do things, and both being OK is the agreement you are both working to.

When you think about setting boundaries, you have to realise that you already have boundaries. You know about them because of that familiar feeling of someone treading on your toes or asking too much of you. If you get any feelings of resentment or you feel that you have been treated unfairly then this is a warning that your boundaries have been pushed. Take these feelings as a sign that helps you to become of where your boundaries are right now. Only then can you decide if these are still right for you.

Pay attention to your gut instincts. When you feel that tension or resentment building, when you want to tell someone to back off, what's really happening? What are you learning about yourself in these moments? Are your boundaries right for you now, or is your autopilot hanging on to out-of-date settings? The feelings you get when your boundaries are pushed aren't telling you what's right and wrong, the feelings are telling you what you are used to. The feelings reveal your habits, your autopilot defaults!

Setting your boundaries

People often have trouble setting their boundaries, feeling that what they want isn't right or fair. A sure sign that they don't see themselves as equals! One of the biggest problems is that people wait until it's too late, they wait until the boundary has been pushed before they reveal that it exists. Imagine visiting a new country and getting arrested by the police for walking on government property, when there are no signs or fences! You would feel unfairly treated, right? And if the police said, "You should have known!" then you would feel that was even more unfair!

If you wait until your boundaries have been pushed, you'll just get into an argument. You'll end up defending yourself, trying to justify why you're upset, it's almost impossible to think clearly. You've taken a simple request and turned it onto a biryani!

The solution is always the same. Use those quick stress reducing tips that I gave you earlier, take time out to breathe and reflect, and then in a calmer, quieter moment, think about how you can assert your boundary and tell the other person in a way that they can respect. Remember, they will respect you when they see that you respect yourself, and the way to do that is by taking ownership of your needs.

Set your boundaries and communicate them to others by starting with "I" not "you". If you say, "You always do this", or, "You always make me angry when you do that", or, "You shouldn't do it that way", then you're sure to start an argument. Instead, say, "I would like you to do this" or "I feel more comfortable when you do it this way".

By starting with "I" you are taking ownership and responsibility. When you start with "you" you're blaming other people for not knowing where your invisible boundaries are!

Your boundaries could be space, time, responsibilities, likes, dislikes... anything that makes you feel relaxed and safe.

You might feel like you have to justify your boundaries. You might say, "I want you to do this, because of X, and Y, and Z". There are no reasons. Your boundaries don't need explaining. If you know someone who always asks you why you like things a certain way, are they testing to see if they can push you a bit further?

You can imagine children being very good at this...

"It's bedtime, go and brush your teeth" ... "Why do I need to brush my teeth?" ... "Because if you don't your teeth will be bad" ... "But why?"

The child draws the parent into a discussion on oral hygiene, and the parent doesn't notice that bedtime just got extended!

Your boundaries need no explanation. You are not asking. You are not negotiating. Your life, your needs, your goals, your boundaries. Other people are free to set theirs, that's the bargain.

Saying no

You have spent your whole life building a system around you, a system that supports your autopilot settings. If you need to feel helpful to people, you'll be surrounded by people who take advantage of your help. If you need to feel smart, you'll be surrounded by people who need to pick your brains. The people and relationships that you've created now have expectations of you. When you decide to change your autopilot settings and redraw your boundaries, one of the most difficult things that you have to do is to reset these external relationships, and that means saying no.

It's easy to say no to simple things, habits that other people already know about. If you take your coffee and someone offers you cream, you can say, "No, thanks" very easily. But what happens when someone is asking for something that you're trying to change in your life? It's much harder to say no when your friends and colleagues are expecting you to say yes, because you always say yes.

Saying no is the easy part, the hard part is dealing with all the repeated requests for you to justify yourself, and of course the biggest obstacle is your fear of conflict. If you explain your reasons, you are showing that you are open to negotiation, that your boundaries are flexible. All the hard work you've put in up to this point will be wasted. When your boundaries are flexible, you are showing people that you are prepared to accept the minimum. If someone offers a car for sale and says they're willing to accept between $10,000 and $15,000, who in their right mind would offer the top end? What would you offer? $11,000? Or would you go right for $10,000 since the seller already said that would be acceptable?

If you're offered a new job, and the hiring manager says that the pay range is $50,000 to $70,000, what would you ask for? Certainly not the lowest figure! Would you go for the highest? Or would you come down a little, maybe $65,000, just to show that you're not greedy?

If you let people know that your boundaries are flexible, don't be surprised when those people test to make sure, and don't be surprised when they expect you to always honour your lowest offer.

Don't let other people push you into saying yes, just because that's what you've always done.

It's easier for you to say yes, just one more time, and promise yourself that next time, it will be different. Of course, next time never comes. You will never find the right time, you have to create the right time.

Mutual respect

One of the most important ways to set your boundaries and take ownership of your life is to respect other people's boundaries too. Don't expect to walk all over other people and then have them come running to meet your needs.

When you show respect for others, you demand respect in return for yourself. Remember, any relationship is a fair and equal exchange. When you take ownership of what you are in control of, and you allow others to do the same from their side, you create clear rules for the relationship and that creates trust. With trust, we can achieve anything.

Questions

✈ What is yours?

✈ How do you feel when someone tries to take what is yours?

✈ Think of a time when you have felt coerced or manipulated. How did you invite this?

✈ When you say 'yes' to someone else, are you saying 'no' to yourself?

✈ How often do you feel that you are compromising?

✈ How do you take responsibility in your life?

✈ How do you avoid responsibility?

✈ How do you hold others to their responsibilities?

✈ How have your boundaries been pushed today?

✈ How did you communicate your boundaries to others?

✈ How does this help you to affirm your boundaries in your life?

✈ How will you communicate this to the people around you?

13

You the Creator

> Life isn't about finding yourself; life is
> about creating yourself
>
> *George Bernard Shaw*

You might think that you can only control so much in your life. You can only eat what the restaurant sells, you can only drive where there are roads, you can only watch what's on TV, you can only do your job in the way your employer wants you to. So your life is a constant balance between what you want and what is available.

What if you had complete control over all of these aspects of your life, and more? What if you could control every detail? What would you do with all of that choice? What would you create that doesn't exist today? What flavours, textures, colours would you create? What would you change in your daily routine?

What would you change in your job, your hobbies, your home, your friends and family?

And what if I told you that all of this is possible?

It becomes possible when you realise that all of these people, places and events aren't 'out there' - they are part of you, inseparable from you. Why? Because what matters isn't these things, people and places, what matters is your experience of them, and your experience of them is entirely created within your mind.

White rice. Boring or comforting? Biryani. Complicated or sophisticated? A normal day at work. Dull or reassuring?

So maybe you cannot change what the world throws at you, but you can choose what it means to you. You can receive every day as a curse or a blessing. You can receive every event as a forfeit or a gift. You can see every person as a barrier or an enabler.

Remember what's happening in your brain. By the time you are consciously aware of what's happening, your brain has already reacted to it. When you train new reactions, new habits, you respond to what's happening around you in a more constructive way. The information which then reaches your neocortex is different. The event itself seems different. That colleague who used to irritate you now seems... softer, somehow. Your reaction when people don't seem to listen to you just seems... gentler, slower, easier. And then you begin to notice the effect on other people too. So creating your reality isn't some esoteric Matrix-style fantasy, because the reality is that you are creating your reality right now!

And now comes the biggest, most difficult, most challenging question of all. If you are creating your reality right now, why would you create bad things, irritating things, problems, mistakes and failures? They must serve some purpose for you, right? Otherwise you would not be creating them!

Some people think that these irritations serve as a message to remind them of the importance of gratitude. Maybe that helps them to stay focused. Some people think that these irritations serve as lessons to help you to learn and grow. Maybe that works for them.

What works for you? Maybe you think you need bad things to happen in your life to convince you that it's real? Maybe if everything in life went your way, you would think it was too good to be true? If that's the case then maybe you make bad things happen? Maybe you make mistakes on purpose!

It's easier to think that bad things happen by accident. It's easier to blame the chef for the biryani. It's easier to think that you're the innocent victim in all of this. If you accept that you create your reality then you become the architect. When things go wrong, it's your fault. It's so much easier to put the blame on others. It's much easier to blame fate.

You are already creating your reality because your brain is editing the information from your senses and your emotional reactions have already happened before your conscious awareness kicks in. So if you really want to begin creating your reality, you have to make new habits.

In 2009 researchers from University College London examined the new habits of 96 people over a 12 week duration. They defined habits as, "Behaviours which are performed automatically because they have been performed frequently in the past. This repetition creates a mental association between the situation (cue) and action (behaviour) which means that when the cue is encountered the behaviour is performed automatically. Automaticity has a number of components, one of which is lack of thought."

Lack of thought? There's the autopilot!

They found an average time it takes for a new habit to stick is 66 days with the full range being from 18 to 254 days. Two factors come in here - the habit and the individual link. Some habits are easy to break, some are more difficult. The outside environment plays a big part. If you're trying to give up smoking and all your friends smoke, it's really hard to say no or to take yourself out of that situation.

To create a habit you need to consciously repeat the behaviour in the same environment or situation so that there's a trigger for the behaviour. You might start your habit after breakfast, or when you hear a certain song, or when you arrive at work. Make the environment part of the habit and your brain will connect the two together.

When you want to break a habit, the easiest way is to create a new one. The brain can't deal with negatives or things that don't exist, so not doing something is the same as doing it. Try as hard as you can to imagine not scratching your nose. Imagine not smiling. Imagine not reading these words. To imagine not doing it you first have to imagine doing it. So when you try to break a habit you are up against two problems. First, you can't think of not doing the habit. Second, by the time you realise you're doing the habit, you have already done it and your conscious mind is just catching up, so by the time you kick yourself it's already too late.

New habits don't stop the old habits, they just have to become stronger influences on your behaviour. In time, the old habit will fade away as you forget it. In a year's time, you won't even remember that you used to do it, until you see an old photo or something reminds you.

What it really comes down to is - how badly do you want that shift in autopilot mode? What will you do to get it? How will you maintain it?

Sometimes, people change the surface layer, the behaviour. Maybe they can maintain that for some time, but the old habit fights back, especially when they're stressed, under pressure or back in some familiar environment.

A change in behaviour is exactly what it is… A change in behaviour. It hasn't affected anything at a deeper level. When your identity is not consistent with your behaviour, you are bound to fail. You will only behave as you want when you're thinking about it, and at other times your autopilot will take over. You'll catch yourself and promise yourself to fix it next time, but that will never happen. You're like an employee who only works when the boss is watching. When the conscious neocortex is focused on the task, the right behaviour comes along. When the autopilot is back in charge, the short cut is the best option.

You cannot live life behaving like someone you are not. Eventually it will flip! Your identity is your story or self-image. You can only be your identity, no-one else's.

There's a model that's often applied to personal change called 'logical levels'. It's based on an observation that when people make changes in their lives, the way they think and talk about that change develops over time and doesn't take place all at once. If you're a parent, when did you become a parent? At the moment of your child's birth, or before, or after? Think about your current job title. When did you move into this role? Did you work for it for a long time, and did you feel that you were really doing the job for a long time before a position became available? Or did you get the job or the promotion and feel out of your depth for a while until you built up your experience and confidence?

Here's an example - the time you passed your driving test.

Identity	I am a driver
Belief	I'm confident in the car
Capability	I can drive
Behaviour	I am learning to drive
Environment	I am in the car

Here's another example.

Identity	I am a chef
Belief	I make good biryani
Capability	I can make biryani
Behaviour	I am making biryani
Environment	I work in the kitchen

Maybe you've seen an old movie where a panicked member of the cabin crew shouted to the passengers, "Can anyone fly a plane?!" Well, someone could sit in the pilot's seat but they're not a pilot. They could even put on the pilot's uniform. They could push a few buttons, maybe make an announcement to the passengers. They could emulate things they've seen on TV, but that doesn't make them a pilot. If you've got children, you'll have seen them playing 'pretend' games. They pretend to be a racing driver or a doctor by copying other people, but they can't copy how someone else thinks. We can't see other people making decisions. OK, so the pilot pressed that button, but when? And why? So lots of experience, trial and error has to happen before a person can think about their capability. Capability requires knowledge, and knowledge requires learning.

The passenger in the movie might follow instructions from the air traffic controller. They might press a button here, pull a lever there. In the movie, they land the plane! They walk away and say, "I did it". They don't say, "Right, I'm a pilot now, where to next?!"

So at the behaviour level, you're focused on what you're doing right now, but just because you're doing something right now doesn't mean that you feel you have the capability. That comes from repeated practice and knowledge, and even from sharing your knowledge with others. To form beliefs, you have to compare yourself to other people. Being able to repeat some behaviour is the first step, but then you have to make that behaviour part of who you are. It becomes part of your identity. You no longer think about driving your car, you just think about where you need to get to. The autopilot takes over! The first step is programming the autopilot.

Put yourself in the right environment with the right people around you, people to learn from and support you.

Becoming who you are was not hard, you learned it didn't you? Who did you learn it from? How did you learn it? When you look in the mirror today, how do you know who you are? You created yourself, but not out of 'thin air'. You built your identity on the foundation of your relationships and life experiences, and you can create and recreate that identity as you wish, and I know this because you already have recreated your identity, and you will continue to do so as your life circumstances change.

The power to create carries great responsibility. When you are free to create yourself, you can't blame anyone else for the way you are, or the way your life has turned out. Everything that happens in your life is because you will it, or you allow it. Nothing happens by accident. When you are the creator, you have responsibility for what you create. That responsibility isn't only to yourself, it is to everyone around you, because the way you live your life makes a difference to other people.

An autopilot can navigate one aircraft, but it doesn't replace air traffic control. The autopilot is not – yet – aware of other aircraft. The autopilot can do a perfect job by itself and still cause a disaster. When we put people in an environment where they have to share and compete for resources, not everything goes to plan. The good news for you is that there is no limit to the amount of success in the world.

If you want to know why something isn't working out for you, look at yourself. Your life isn't testing you, it is only reflecting you. The world that you have created around you is a reflection of you. You see what you want to see, and you experience events as you expect them to be. You expect to have a bad day at work? You'll make it happen. You expect to have a great night out with friends? It is inevitable.

To create yourself you will need commitment, so if you are not committed, don't waste your time here. Read another book, buy another course, attend a new training and hope that one day the answers you seek will magically appear with no effort on your part.

Changing yourself is as easy as changing your mind about what to order for lunch. Ordering something different instead of 'the usual' - that's the hard part. Making that change real in the world, that's even harder. I'm not trying to put you off, I'm letting you know that there's some work to do, it doesn't just happen by itself. Change happens because you make it happen. Most importantly, change becomes permanent in your life when you change the system around you, the relationships, places, routines that keep pushing your autopilot back to its old settings. Be kind to yourself, and let your friends and family support you by telling them what you're aiming for. Of course, this is a scary step. You don't want to tell other people because you don't want to admit that there was something that needed to change. You just want to turn up one day as the new, perfect you. What you need to understand is that they already know, and they accept you for it anyway. When you finally commit to change, you're usually the last person to realise it.

As you prepare for the journey of a lifetime, here's a simple procedure to help you on your way.

1. Find a behaviour that you want to change.

2. Consider the kind of person who would behave like this.

3. Identify the events which trigger this behaviour.

4. Choose an alternative behaviour - not better, just different.

5. When you are aware of the triggering events, consciously test out the new behaviour and notice how proud you can be of your hard work.

6. When you catch yourself in the old behaviour, acknowledge the wonderful power of your mind and be proud of yourself for noticing, and then switch to the new behaviour.

7. Ask the people around you to support and help you reinforce the change by catching examples of your old behaviour, or the triggers for it.

8. If your old behaviour was harmful to someone else, apologise to them sincerely - get used to saying "I'm sorry" and "I was wrong".

9. Keep practising this until you catch yourself using the new behaviour in place of the old one. Notice how the repetitive change in behaviour alters your

identity. When you can no longer identify with the old, your autopilot mode has shifted.

10. Reward yourself for your success in resetting your autopilot.

And always remember - it's not happy people who are grateful, it's grateful people who are happy.

Questions

- ✈ Are you ready to be fully responsible for your life?
- ✈ Given the power to create, what can you finally let go of?
- ✈ What do you now realise you have been afraid of?
- ✈ What was that fear based on?
- ✈ Are you ready to be your true, authentic self?
- ✈ How do you define yourself?
- ✈ What is unique about you?
- ✈ What qualities and abilities have brought you this far in life?
- ✈ What qualities and abilities are important for the next stage of your life journey?
- ✈ How will you develop these qualities and abilities?
- ✈ Who will help you with this?
- ✈ How will you ask for help in this?
- ✈ What do you believe is your true potential?
- ✈ When you have achieved this true potential, what next?
- ✈ What have you learned on this journey so far?
- ✈ How will you use your knowledge to help others on the same journey?
- ✈ As a result of all of this, who have you become?
- ✈ And who will you be tomorrow?

Simpli*fly*

14

About Mark Dias

Mark Dias is an accomplished, innovative, learning specialist who has partnered with numerous airlines to deliver a variety of training and mentoring programs. Mark entered the aviation industry at 20 years old, working in cabin crew roles for a number of major airlines.

In 2006 Mark entered the world of Human Factors and Crew Resource Management, it is from here on that he found his passion for the development of human behaviour. Working mainly in the Middle East, Mark spent two years working as a cabin safety instructor before moving back into the field of crew resource management and human performance limitations. Mark has an extensive aviation training history including qualifications in Training Human

Factors and Crew Resource Management, Instructor Assessments and Training and Course design.

Alongside his extensive aviation career, Mark completed courses in Investigating Human Performance, Human Factors IATA, and Train the Trainers. Mark has further training in NLP, coaching and personal development.

Mark is based somewhere between Vancouver and Dubai and devotes his time to coaching and mentoring using his unique formula as explored in this book. Mark has channelled his expertise in aviation into his performance coaching with great success, working with clients across the world from many different walks of life.

Connect with Mark via LinkedIn or visit his website:

www.markdias.co

www.ingramcontent.com/pod-product-compliance
Lightning Source LLC
Chambersburg PA
CBHW021930040426
42448CB00008B/989